The Arapaho Indians

The Arapaho Indians

A RESEARCH GUIDE AND BIBLIOGRAPHY

Compiled by ZDENĚK SALZMANN

Bibliographies and Indexes in Anthropology, Number 4

GREENWOOD PRESS
NEW YORK • WESTPORT, CONNECTICUT • LONDON

Library of Congress Cataloging-in-Publication Data

Salzmann, Zdeněk.
  The Arapaho Indians : a research guide and bibliography / compiled
by Zdeněk Salzmann.
      p.   cm.—(Bibliographies and indexes in anthropology, ISSN
0742-6844; no. 4)
  Includes index.
  ISBN 0-313-25354-4 (lib. bdg. : alk. paper)
  1. Arapaho Indians—Bibliography.   2. Arapaho Indians—Archives—
Directories.   3. Arapaho Indians—Museums—Directories.   I. Title.
II. Series.
Z1210.A67S25   1988
[E99.A7]
016.973′0497—dc19   87-32274

British Library Cataloguing in Publication Data is available.

Library of Congress Catalog Card Number: 87-32274
ISBN: 0-313-25354-4
ISSN: 0742-6844

First published in 1988

Greenwood Press, Inc.
88 Post Road West, Westport, Connecticut 06881

Printed in the United States of America

The paper used in this book complies with the
Permanent Paper Standard issued by the National
Information Standards Organization (Z39.48-1984).

10 9 8 7 6 5 4 3 2 1

Contents

Preface

This research guide and bibliography directs those interested in the culture and history of the Arapaho Indians to over 1350 pertinent publications, archival sources, and museum collections. It is hoped that this compilation will also be of help to the Arapaho themselves as they strive to preserve their cultural heritage and identity.

Among similar works, the present volume stands out by its unusually broad scope, referring the user not only to books, articles, and dissertations, but to public documents and depositories of manuscripts and collections of material culture as well. The result is a very comprehensive reference indeed, but it is precisely the ambitious scope of the work that makes completeness an elusive goal and the volume quite likely subject to minor additions and further improvements in subsequent editions. The compiler therefore welcomes suggestions from users as to how to make this research guide and bibliography even more helpful.

The work consists of four parts: a historical and ethnographic sketch of the Arapaho Indians (pp. 1-12); the bibliography, preceded by an overview of the most important sources and followed by a topical index (pp. 13-61); several reference lists with information concerning the Arapaho Indians to be found in the public documents of the United States (pp. 63-100); and directories of archives and museums with significant collections pertaining to the Arapaho (pp. 101-113).

Joy Salzmann must be thanked for the patient and painstaking work it has taken to prepare the accurate copy from which this book has been reproduced.

The Arapaho Indians

The Arapaho: A Historical and Ethnographic Sketch

The following historical and ethnographic sketch of the Arapaho is no more than the title promises--a sketch. Its sole purpose is to assist the user of this research guide and bibliography in pursuing topics of specialized interest with a better understanding of the general context of Arapaho history and culture.

The first part of the sketch deals with the ethnohistory of the Arapaho, both Northern and Southern, up to the time when they had to give up their free-roaming life as hunters on the Great Plains and settle in locations assigned to them by the United States government. Their subsequent struggle to adjust to the new circumstances--the process of profound and traumatic culture change--has been too complex to do justice to in a few paragraphs. Fortunately, there are a number of sources that deal with several aspects of their adjustment.

The second part of the sketch gives a brief account of the Arapaho culture approximately as of the time of initial white contact. In this part, too, only selected topics have been accorded treatment, with occasional references to the contemporary situation. The reader should keep in mind that there is no substitute for the study of primary sources, which over the past hundred years have come to include some truly outstanding works on both the history of the Arapaho and various aspects of their culture.

☆   ☆   ☆

The Arapaho people, who today live both in Wyoming (the Northern Arapaho) and Oklahoma (the Southern Arapaho), were not always roaming the western plains of North America in pursuit of the buffalo. While archaeological excavations have thus far thrown little if any light on the prehistory of the Arapaho, linguistic research has provided some valuable clues concerning their geographic origin. As an Algonquian language, Arapaho belongs to a family of related languages extending in modern times from Labrador and the northern Atlantic coast in the east to Montana in the west. As a result of painstaking comparative research in the history of the language family, solid evidence has been advanced indicating that the ancestral language spoken by the ancient Algonquians some two to three thousand years ago was limited to an area bounded by Lake Huron in the west, the Ottawa River in the north, and Lake Ontario in the south. From this ancient homeland, one group after another moved out in many directions, these migrations eventually giving rise to separate Algonquian-speaking tribes, each with its own distinct language, Arapaho among them.

It is much more difficult to attempt to answer the question as to when and by what route the westward migration of those who were to become the modern Arapaho took place. There are two main theories concerning the prehistoric movements of these people.

According to one, the Arapaho must have been separated from their eastern relatives for at least a thousand years and become established on the Plains during the first half of the present millennium. According to the alternate theory, influenced in part by some tenuous bits of oral tradition, the Arapaho gave up their horticultural economy and abandoned their earth-lodge villages just west of the Great Lakes to move in a southwesterly direction, crossing the Missouri River probably sometime after 1600 or possibly even later, and in a relatively short time becoming completely dependent on the buffalo in the area of the Great Plains. Such a profound change in their mode of living would have been made possible by the northward spread of the horse, introduced in its modern form to the New World by the Spaniards during the early sixteenth century. The difficulty in choosing between these and other reconstructions of Arapaho prehistory stems from the fact that historical sources do not begin to make clear references to the Arapaho until relatively late. Lack of historical records may be taken to suggest that either the migration of the Arapaho took place before that of the Cheyenne and Blackfeet, about whom written records are not as silent, or that the Arapaho took a northern route to reach the Great Plains and by so doing remained largely unnoticed.

In any case, the presence of the Arapaho west of the Missouri River is not conclusively documented until the end of the eighteenth century, by which time they began to be referred to as having hunted in an area extending from present-day northwestern Montana to western South Dakota and Nebraska and as far south as the Arkansas River in Colorado. During the next several decades, they tended to move in a southerly direction, their southernmost excursions reaching the Comanche and Kiowa Apache country in Texas, from where they were said periodically to visit Kansas and Colorado to raid and trade. By the mid-nineteenth century, the bulk of the tribe, together with the Cheyenne, had established hunting grounds in what today are southeastern Wyoming and the northeastern part of Colorado.

Prior to any significant impact of white people on the northern Plains, the Arapaho were wholly dependent on the buffalo for both food and material for shelter and clothing as well as a great many other objects of daily use. The buffalo herds were huge and the tribes who followed them were generally assured an adequate harvest.

The seeds of eventual change were introduced when the Great Plains tribes acquired the horse (in the case of the Arapaho sometime between 1700 and 1750) and a short time later the gun, both of which made buffalo hunting much more efficient. The change was accelerated after 1820 by the growing trade in buffalo hides, which caused many more animals to be killed than was necessary for the Indians' subsistence. The most ominous development, however, took place during the 1840s when increasing numbers of white settlers began crossing the Plains, destroying grazing lands, frightening away the game, and spreading diseases against which the native inhabitants had no immunity. According to estimates made during the summer of 1845 by Colonel Stephen W. Kearney, who together with 250 dragoons was sent on a show-of-strength expedition along the Platte River trail leading to Oregon, he encountered no fewer than 2,325 people, 460 wagons, 7,000 head of cattle, and 400 horses and mules. Travel on the Oregon and Santa Fe trails intensified after the discovery in 1848 of gold in far-off California. To minimize the conflict between the Indians and whites, and to insure the safe passage of settlers along the main westward routes, in 1849 the commissioner of Indian affairs instructed the superintendent of Indian affairs at Saint Louis and Indian Agent Thomas Fitzpatrick to make peace and conclude a treaty with the Plains tribes. When on August 31, 1851, the two officials arrived at Fort Laramie, where the treaty council was to be held, they found some ten thousand Indians waiting for them, including a large contingent of the Arapaho.

Among the various provisions of this first of several treaties concluded by the United States and the Arapaho, they and the Cheyenne were assigned the territory between the North Platte and the Arkansas rivers, including most of today's Colorado east of the Rocky Mountains as well as adjoining parts of present-day Wyoming, Nebraska, and Kansas.

The treaty notwithstanding, the fate of the Arapaho as free-roaming hunters was rapidly approaching a tragic conclusion. The buffalo herds were steadily diminishing while at the same time the movements of the Arapaho were becoming severely circumscribed by the towns springing up throughout the prairie as a result of the gold rush in 1858 in the Pikes Peak region south of Denver, close to the heart of Arapaho country.

As Indian-white hostilities intensified, the northerly bands of the Arapaho sought refuge and traditional subsistence farther to the north, while members of the

southerly division remained in present-day Colorado even after having been restricted by an invalid treaty in 1861 to a greatly reduced area along the upper
Arkansas River and its tributary Big Sandy Creek.

In 1865, a year after a congressional inquiry into the tragic encounter at
Sand Creek between the Indians and the troops of Colonel J. M. Chivington condemned
the action as a "wholesale massacre of Arapahos and Cheyennes...[who] were there en-
camped under the direction of our officers, and believed themselves to be under the
protection of our flag," the southern bands of the Arapaho and Cheyenne were prom-
ised a small reservation in southern Kansas and the adjacent part of Indian Territory. However, because Kansas had refused to permit the establishment of an Indian
reservation within its boundaries, in 1867 the Arapaho and Cheyenne were assigned to
an area between the Arkansas and Cimarron rivers in the Cherokee Outlet along the
northern boundary of present-day Oklahoma. Dissatisfied with the location, the
Indians refused to settle on the land. Finally, by an executive order in 1869
President Grant set aside a new reservation site for the two tribes below the Cherokee Outlet, along the North Canadian and upper Washita rivers. Although this area
was to become the permanent home of the Southern Arapaho, it was not to remain altogether theirs--a portion of it was sheared away a few years later to serve other
displaced Native Americans. Moreover, in the early 1890s the Southern Arapaho and
Cheyenne had to give up communal owning of land in favor of individual plots, and
their reservation was then thrown open to white settlement.

The fortunes of the northern bands of the Arapaho, who had never formally given
up their rights to their traditional Colorado hunting grounds, proved to be no less
tragic. Except for the period of about 1864 to 1868, when they allied themselves
with the Cheyenne and the Sioux, the Arapaho through their intermediaries made several attempts to come to reasonable terms with the United States government, having
suffered considerable losses both in encounters with the military and from smallpox
and cholera. In 1867 they began appealing to the authorities for a reservation they
could call their own.

When in 1868 the Northern Arapaho and Cheyenne met at Fort Laramie with government representatives to negotiate a new treaty, the Indians had little choice but to
accept terms stipulating, among other conditions, that they settle outside Colorado
in one of several possible locations. None held much appeal for the Arapaho, whose
preference was to be assigned a permanent home in present-day Wyoming. Although in
1870 an attempt of the Northern Arapaho to share a reservation east of the Wind
River Range with their traditional enemies, the Shoshone, had lasted only a few
months, the Northern Arapaho were nevertheless permanently assigned to the Wind
River Reservation in 1878. Over 3 million acres in area in 1868, by 1904 the reservation had shrunk to a little over 800,000 acres, but a substantial portion of the
land was later restored. At present nearly 1.9 million acres in extent, it continues
to be the home of the Northern Arapaho as well as the Shoshone, who had preceded them
there by a decade.

By the time the Northern Arapaho found their permanent home, the slaughter of
the buffalo had grown to ruinous proportions. Estimates put it at over 4 million
head between 1872 and 1874 in the central Plains, followed by the extermination of
the herds in the southern Plains (Texas and Indian Territory) between 1874 and 1877,
as well as hundreds of thousands more in the northern Plains in the early 1880s.
A certain Orlando A. Bond in 1876 killed three hundred buffalo on a particularly suc-
cessful day, and he averaged about one hundred killings a day in order to keep five
skinners busy.

Although residing and hunting in different parts of the Great Plains prior to
the 1860s, the members of the northern and southern bands used to come together for
annual ritual observances. In less than a generation they had become separated from
each other by a distance of some eight hundred miles, and even though a great deal of
contact between them continued on an individual basis, they began evolving under
quite different conditions as two separate political entities.

                              *   *   *

One of the founders of American anthropology, A. L. Kroeber, received his initiation into fieldwork among the Southern Arapaho in Indian Territory (later Oklahoma) in 1899 and a year later among the Northern Arapaho in Wyoming. Although by that time their old way of life was in complete disarray, its former vibrancy and dignity were still within living memory. It is especially to Kroeber that we are indebted for our knowledge of what Arapaho traditional culture must have been like during the period when the encroachment of the white settlers from the East was only just beginning to be felt.

The lifeway of Plains Indians, and therefore also of the Arapaho, has occasionally been referred to as a buffalo culture because the buffalo (<u>Bison</u> <u>bison</u>) was not only the principal source of their subsistence but the focal point of their material culture, having been utilized with amazing completeness. Some of the flesh, as well as the brain, tongue, and blood, was consumed soon after the animal was killed; the remaining meat was processed for future use, for example, as pemmican. Blood was also used as a curative agent, and the brains in tanning skins.

Buffalo rawhide was used for a variety of objects ranging from containers of varied shapes and functions to saddles, ropes, stirrups, shields, eating plates, and bullboats, while the softer skin obtained by tanning served for the manufacture of blankets, robes, various articles of clothing, laces, quivers, tipi covers and liners, cradles, sweat-lodge covers, and toys. The horns were used in medicine, as containers, and for headdresses, while the skull of the animal, painted, played an important role in the annual sun-dance ritual. Tufts of buffalo beard and the animal's teeth were used for ornamentation; the tendons for bowstrings, thread, and glue; hair for headdresses, cordage, and ornaments, but primarily as a filler for pads, pillows, balls, and dolls. Depending on their shape, buffalo bones were the source of a great variety of tools and utensils for daily use--fleshing tools, pipes, knives, scrapers, saddletrees, spades, war clubs, jewelry, arrowheads, and others. Even internal organs proved serviceable as pouches, bags, or cooking vessels. Dewclaws were used as rattles or decorations; hoofs for glue; tails for brushes, whips, or medicine switches; the rough surface of the tongue for hairbrushes or combs; and the fat for cooking, soap, hair grease, and cosmetic and decorative aids, especially body paints. Finally, dried buffalo dung, known as buffalo chips, served as fuel and, when finely ground, as diaper powder to prevent chafing, as well as for other medicinal purposes.

This detailed account of the Arapaho utilization of the natural commissary available to them in the Plains has been presented not only to demonstrate the ingenious adaptation the Arapaho made with respect to the main natural resource of the area but to point out the despair in which they must have found themselves when in the short span of a generation the vast buffalo herds were destroyed under their very eyes.

While buffalo meat served as a staple, elk, deer, and antelope were enjoyed, and dog meat, especially from puppies, was considered a delicacy. Among other foods were wild roots and a variety of wild fruits--especially wild cherries, buffalo berries, and wild currants.

The chief occupation of Arapaho men was the chase. Before the adoption of horses, small groups of buffalo were enticed or stampeded into enclosures and shot at close range; alternately, buffalo were rounded up by firing prairie grass. Once horses had been acquired, the collective hunts usually took the form of either driving herds over a cliff, or surrounding smaller numbers of buffalo and shooting them with bows and arrows from horseback. Arapaho men were also expected to make and decorate their own gear and weapons and to care for their horses.

Women's duties consisted of gathering and preparing food, including digging up wild roots and collecting berries, dressing skins and making and maintaining clothing, and putting up and taking down family tepees. Before the introduction of the horse, burdens were transported from place to place on dog-pulled travois consisting of two trailing poles serving as shafts with a platform or net between them to carry the load. When horses began to be used as draft animals, travois became larger and more efficient.

The Northern Arapaho were divided into four named bands, each of which was led by a chief and made up of a group of extended households based on matrilocal residence. The bands hunted and camped independently of each other in their favorite

locations, but joined together during the summer for communal hunting and tribal
ceremonies. At that time, members of each band were assigned a definite position
in the camp circle, which took the form of an east-facing C.

Arapaho kinship terms were and continue to be of the classificatory type, meaning that certain lineal and collateral relatives are terminologically lumped together.
For example, an individual's father, his brother(s), mother's sister's husband, and
certain other kin are referred to by the same kinship term; a similar terminological
relationship exists in the case of an individual's mother, her sister(s), father's
brother's wife, and so on. On the other hand, mother's brother(s) and father's
sister(s) are referred to by separate terms, roughly corresponding to English
"uncle" and "aunt." Grandparents, as well as all of their siblings and their
spouses, are subsumed under two terms, according to the gender of the person. Both
a man's own children and the children of his classificatory brothers (who in our
terms would include male cousins) are terminologically his sons and daughters, those
of a man's classificatory sister(s) his nephews and nieces. A corresponding arrangement obtains for the children of a woman and her classificatory sisters on the one
hand and her classificatory brothers on the other. All children in the second descending generation from an individual, regardless of the degree of relationship and
gender, are classified by the term equivalent to the English "grandchild." Affinal
relatives, those based on marriage, are separately designated. One interesting
feature of the Arapaho kinship system is the existence of certain terminological relationships that suggest that at some time in their more distant past the Arapaho
practiced preferential cross-cousin marriage--the custom that an individual marry,
if possible, the child of a parent's sibling of the opposite gender (for example, a
father's sister's child or a mother's brother's child).

A person's attitude and behavior toward kin designated by the same term were
similar. In addition, certain pairs of relatives were subject to restrictions on
behavior or, conversely, encouraged toward familiarity. For example, a very strict
rule of mutual avoidance governed the relationship between a man and his mother-in-
law; by contrast a man was expected to indulge in "rough" joking with his brothers-
and sisters-in-law; grandparents and grandchildren treated each other with affection
and indulged in joking and mutual teasing.

The typical marriage was validated by an exchange of goods between the families
of the couple, but at times a young man was accepted by the bride's father as a
prospective son-in-law when he obligated himself to work for the father for a period
of up to several years. Polygyny was allowed and both sororate and levirate were
practiced. In the former arrangement a man was married to women who were sisters,
either simultaneously or after the death of a first wife. In levirate, a widow was
taken by a brother of her deceased husband. Divorces were fairly common and usually
resulted from incompatibility or the wife's infidelity.

Upon reaching their upper teens, Arapaho men were expected to become members of
a system of eight peer-graded societies, or lodges, with military, social, educational, and ceremonial functions. Membership in the lodges was progressive; one began
at the bottom, among the so-called Kit-Fox Men, and advanced with others to the next
degree. The last two degrees consisted of old men, and the highest of the eight,
the so-called Water-Sprinkling Old Men, had a highly restricted membership and enjoyed the greatest respect. Each society had its own distinct organization and ceremonial observances, and members of the various lodges were called upon to render a
variety of services during religious rituals, hunting expeditions, war parties, when
the tribe was on the march, and around the camp circle.

Women were served by only one society, the Buffalo Lodge; a woman's position
derived primarily from the social standing of her husband.

Small-scale warfare was one of the major activities in the life of Arapaho men,
who in following the buffalo would on occasion run into bands from hostile tribes.
Bravery and risk-taking were valued more than expediency: striking a living enemy
carried far more prestige than killing him, as did the capture of horses from inside an enemy camp. Acquisition of territory was not the reason for raids; an economic motive was added only after the introduction of the horse, which among the
Plains Indians became the most valuable form of property. The recounting of exploits and acts of bravery at any major gathering was an occasion for members of the
societies to gain recognition for themselves and their lodges. Any truly outstanding individuals were sought out at these times to serve as sponsors in name-giving

ceremonies for children and to perform important functions in tribal rituals.

As an institutionalized system of attitudes toward, beliefs in, and practices having to do with the supernatural, religion profoundly affected the daily life of the Arapaho. It was based on the belief in an all-pervading force that exercised a controlling influence not only over individuals but over the tribe as a whole. The three principal means of harnessing supernatural power and securing blessings for one's life, family, and undertakings were the individual experience known as the vision quest, respect for sacred tribal objects, and participation in ceremonial events, especially the sun dance.

Only some adult males fasted solitarily on a hilltop or along a stream, usually for four days, seeking an experience known as the vision quest. The personal "medicine," or guardian spirit, that appeared in the dreams of such an individual was most frequently a small animal. Some part of that particular animal, for example, its skin or tail, would then be procured and used in making the man's medicine bag. Amulets were also commonly worn, usually on bracelets or armlets, and ranged from turtle tails, deer fetlocks, horse teeth, and plumes to small humanlike figures made of skin.

The most sacred object of the Arapaho was and continues to be the Flat Pipe. While it belongs to the entire tribe and serves as the symbol of its existence and as guarantor of its safety, the Pipe is in the custody of a designated keeper from among the Northern Arapaho. In the old times, the Flat Pipe was considered too holy to be transported on horseback or travois, and its keeper was expected to hand-carry it in its bundle together with the four poles that form the stand. During the sun dance the bundle containing the Flat Pipe is placed in the ceremonial lodge, where it is venerated, but the Pipe itself is not put on display.

The Flat Pipe is seen only on very rare occasions, marked by an elaborate ceremony lasting several hours. One such occasion, during the mid-1930s, was described in considerable detail by a white man, John G. Carter. According to him, the Flat Pipe is about 15 inches in length and is made of a single piece of what appears to be stone of reddish color. Among the many required elements attendant to the opening of the Flat Pipe bundle and the rewrapping of the Pipe, after all those who are allowed to view the ritual and to touch the Pipe have done so, is a feast given in honor of the Pipe.

The Southern Arapaho have the Sacred Wheel as their holy symbol. The manner of its keeping and the ceremonies surrounding its special viewings are comparable to those of the Flat Pipe.

In the rich ceremonial life of the Arapaho, the so-called sun dance--more appropriately termed offerings lodge--has been the most elaborate and important event because it is observed by the tribe as a whole. Taking place as a rule every summer, the sun dance is celebrated in a roughly circular lodge about fifty feet in diameter erected around a center pole ceremonially felled and raised several days before the dance itself begins. The male dancers who participate in the ritual abstain from food and drink for three full days in fulfillment of a vow to take part in the sun dance in return for supernatural help when all human efforts have seemed insufficient. Apart from being a ritual occasion of the highest importance, the dance brings together most of the Northern Arapaho families as well as visitors from Oklahoma, and thus it serves both as a social reunion and as an important means of reinforcing tribal solidarity.

Members of all societies manufacture objects necessary for daily living, whether containers, clothes, or weapons to hunt with. When an object is finished with greater care than is needed for achieving its practical purpose, one speaks of art.

Among the Arapaho, decorative art was well developed. In earlier times, a great many objects of daily use were decorated, among them tepees, leanbacks (backrests), pillows, moccasins, leggings, belts, shirts, sunshades (crownless hats), headdresses, robes, anklets, armlets, navel amulets, cradles, knife and awl cases, shields, rattles, workbags, parfleches (folded cases from rawhide), and various kinds of pouches to hold porcupine quills, beads, paints, medicine, pipe and tobacco, grooming implements, and the like.

The Arapaho practiced decorative art similar to that of the other Plains tribes as to the materials used and the techniques applied. There were two main types of decoration, embroidery and painting. In embroidery, porcupine quills and, to a lesser extent, plant fibers (for example, corn husks) were used. The main techniques of quilling were wrapping, sewing, braiding, and weaving. By the beginning of this century, beads were in much more common use than quills, which today are virtually unavailable.

Although glass beads, originally made in Venice, Italy, were brought to America by the earliest European explorers, it was not until the end of the eighteenth century that beads came to be known in the West. The first type, the "pony bead," was almost always blue or white and did not reach the Plains in quantity until about 1800. Later during that century "pony beads" were replaced by tiny "cut" beads and "seed" beads of various sizes.

The second method of decorating hides was to paint them with designs. Designs on parfleches and other rawhide articles were applied by incising, scraping, or painting. The painted designs, which were by far the more common, were applied with various sorts of brushes after the outline of the design had been drawn in with a pointed tool. The colors used were red, blue, green, yellow, black, and brown. Originally they were prepared from earths of different colors, charcoal, or plants, and were often mixed with grease.

The distinguishing feature of Arapaho decorative art was its geometric character: most of the lines of embroidered designs were straight, forming triangles and rectangles of various sorts, rhombi, and bands (stripes). Circles were used less frequently, floral designs never. Painted designs were largely restricted to triangles, rectangles, and bands except on shields and shield covers, where animals and other subjects were portrayed with some degree of realism. Designs traditionally had symbolic value, that is, they stood for or suggested something else by virtue of resemblance, relationship, or convention. For example, an equilateral triangle might stand for a mountain if it pointed upward, or for the heart if it pointed downward. Consequently, designs were not applied to objects without thought; rather, they were used to tell a story or to refer to something the Arapaho were acquainted with from nature or their own culture.

Much of the time colors, too, had a general symbolic meaning: red stood for humans, blood, paint, earth, sunset, or rocks; yellow for sunlight, day, or earth; green for vegetation; blue for the sky, haze, mist, fog, distant mountains, or night; and white, besides serving as the normal background, denoted snow, sand, earth, or water.

Few symbols, however, had one meaning only. Each of the various items (animals, natural features, man-made objects, and abstract notions) could be represented by several different symbols, and the use of symbols was not necessarily consistent even in the work of the same individual.

Beading continues to be an active craft among the Arapaho to the present day and is done primarily, though not exclusively, by women. Although traditional geometric patterns still predominate, the decorative repertory has been expanded to include such realistic designs as flowers and animals. The symbolism of the various geometric designs, still widely used and appreciated at the turn of the century, is today no longer known or understood even by the beadworkers of the oldest generation.

Music used to play, and continues to play, an important role in the life of the Arapaho. The emphasis has always been on vocal music--on singing. Although Arapaho songs are monophonic, their style is fairly complex. They have a strophic structure, their melodic contour is descending over several successive phrases. The Arapaho singing voice is characterized by noticeable vocal tension and intensity, and longer tones are marked by heavy pulsation. The majority of the songs are sung with meaningless syllables, but there is a respectable body of songs with texts as well. The largest body of musical material was associated with religion and war; in addition there were many songs used on various social occasions and during gambling. The repertory of love songs, lullabies, and hunting songs was limited.

Men have always been much more active in music than women. It is they who invariably lead the singing and only they play musical instruments. Because of the

limited number of instruments traditionally found among the Arapaho and the other
Plains Indians, purely instrumental performances were very rare. Among the few
instruments the Arapaho did possess were several varieties of rattles made from
materials ranging from rawhide to dried buffalo scrotum. In recent times rattles
have been made from gourds. Bells, which today dancers tie to various parts of
their outfits, were introduced relatively recently. Almost all singing is accompanied by the beat of a drum. The most common type is a round, single-headed drum
about a foot and a half in diameter, accommodating several drummers at the same time;
the drum used in the sun dance usually has two heads. Songs sung in peyote ceremonies are accompanied by a small kettledrum filled partly or completely with water
in order to keep the drumhead moist and the pitch level in the proper range.

There is evidence that in earlier times Arapaho men, when courting a girl,
would at times play on a flageolet; this small flutelike instrument with about a
half dozen finger holes was the only solo instrument used by the Arapaho. One-tone
whistles, originally made of eagle bone, are still common, and are employed both by
sun dancers and those taking part in peyote meetings. Children, especially boys,
used to amuse themselves with bull-roarers consisting of a flat piece of material
(bone or wood) attached to a thong that was swung rapidly in a circular motion to
produce a roaring or humming sound similar to a strong wind.

Social and competitive Indian dancing is one of the favorite pastimes of contemporary Arapaho, both young and adult, male and female, and the musical accompani-
ment without which such events would be unthinkable has served to keep many of the
traditional songs alive. Of what little is left of the traditional culture, Arapaho
music is, along with religion, with which it has close ties, among the best pre-
served elements.

The telling of tales is undoubtedly almost as ancient as language itself and
there is no society on earth whose members, especially the youngest, do not like to
listen to a good storyteller who is able to satisfy their yearnings for excitement,
entertainment, and knowledge. The Arapaho, who like other North American Indians
did not have writing, possessed a wealth of traditional stories, some short and
humorous, others complex enough to require the better part of an hour or more to
tell. There was a time, certainly still when Kroeber was doing his pioneering research at the turn of the century, when storytelling played an important educational
role in the culture. Arapaho children could hardly wait for evening to come, as
that was when they gathered in the tepees--especially in wintertime--and listened to
their grandparents as they taught them by means of traditional stories not only the
do's and don'ts of their culture but also the complexities of their language. Things
have changed a great deal since those times. Many distractions have come along to
claim children's attention, from comic strips and books before World War II to tele-
vision after. Although many children today, and even their parents, know only very
little of their own oral "literature," it is fortunate that some two hundred Arapaho
tales have been recorded, some of them in the original language.

Arapaho tales fall into several categories, very much like those of other Native
American peoples. The most sacred group consists of creation myths that tell of the
origin of the earth and the creation and conditioning of men and animals. Very popu-
lar is a group of tales concerned with the exploits of culture heroes who are subject
to dangerous tests and must overcome monsters or seemingly invincible adversaries.
A clear distinction between events of this world and of others, and between humans
on the one hand and animals on the other, is not maintained in Arapaho tales. This
is evident from stories concerning journeys to the other world, as when in the tale
known as Star Husband a girl wishes to marry a star and finds herself enticed to the
sky where her husband-to-be lives. Similarly, there are numerous tales of humans
married to animal spouses who on occasion appear in human guise.

One of the most characteristic features of Arapaho, and North American, oral
tradition is the presence and great popularity of trickster stories. The most common character in these short tales--comparable to our jokes--is nih?óóθoo, Whiteman,
a mischievous supernatural being who enjoys deceiving others. However, he is not
the only trickster, and is frequently outsmarted by the coyote.

Arapaho stories had much to teach the members of their society: about the need
to conserve natural resources and live in harmony with nature; about the interdepen-
dence between humans and animals; about behaviors that the society could not condone;

and many other lessons. Among contemporary Arapaho nothing so far has been able to replace adequately these traditional narratives as a source of time-tested wisdom.

Arapaho is a member of one of the largest language families in North America, the Algonquian family. The other member languages include Delaware, Natick and Narraganset, Penobscot and Abnaki, Malecite and Passamaquoddy, and Micmac in the Northeast; Shawnee, Fox, Menomini, Potawatomi, Cree, and Ojibwa in the Middle West and central Canada; and Cheyenne, Blackfoot, and Arapaho in the western Plains. Closely related to Arapaho is Atsina, also known as Gros Ventre, at the present actively spoken by only a handful of old-timers in northeastern Montana, where the Atsina live. Because of the structural proximity of the speech of the Atsina to Arapaho proper, it appears that the two peoples must have descended from the same ancestral group and have split off from it only a few centuries ago.

As an Algonquian language, Arapaho has certain characteristic grammatical features, among them a highly inflected verb and complex derivational morphology; a formal distinction between animate and inanimate genders--the former referring to most living things as well as to some others classified by the Arapaho as living (for example, rock, tepee pole, and rope); the distinction in the first person plural of verbs and possessed nouns between exclusive and inclusive forms, the former being employed when the addressee is not among the persons referred to, as when a woman in the presence of her husband talks to a visitor about "our children," who clearly are not the visitor's children (by contrast, inclusive forms subsume the addressee, or hearer, among the persons referred to); the obviative, marking a form or construction, whether in singular or plural, that relates to the subordinate of two animate third person referents in a given context (as in "her horse" or "the chief's son," where "horse" and "son" would appear in the obviative form); and dependency (obligatory possession) of certain nouns, especially body parts and kinship terms--that is, their occurrence exclusively in possessed forms (someone's heart, my heart, my father, your mother, and so on) rather than also in absolute forms (dog, rope, and so on).

The Arapaho vocabulary is very rich and nuanced and is capable and ready to generate terms for new concepts that have entered the Arapaho cultural universe from the outside (words for automobile, radio, and the like). Whereas before World War II most adult Arapaho, at least in Wyoming, either spoke Arapaho actively or understood when it was spoken to them, the number of Arapaho speakers has now declined dramatically to such an extent that the younger generations are for all practical purposes monolingual in English. Moreover, English has even come to influence the speech of those individuals who have managed to retain command of their native language. In short, Arapaho is no longer a flourishing or enduring language; rather, it is a rapidly declining language that has reached the initial stages of obsolescence. The only individuals among the Northern Arapaho who have full command of their language, even if they no longer use it habitually, are members of the oldest generation, which means that parents do not teach Arapaho to their children in the home. As a result, the numbers of active speakers and of those who have some passive knowledge of Arapaho are declining very rapidly: English is preferred in essentially all situations, including even some traditional ceremonial contexts, and the language is losing its communicative viability--its capacity to adapt successfully to new situations--not because of some inherent deficiency but as a result of disuse. Unless a prompt and massive revitalization and restoration program is undertaken, the rich and vibrant language of the Arapaho will cease to be spoken altogether within a generation or so.

*   *   *

The number of individuals who at present consider themselves Arapaho is not easy to establish. Not all of those who could qualify as Southern Arapaho live in the Cheyenne-Arapaho "country" of west-central Oklahoma, but a reasonable estimate of the southern branch can be put at about 3,000. A count of the Northern Arapaho residing on the Wind River Reservation in Wyoming is also difficult to arrive at. In the mid-1980s there were about 3,500 persons on tribal rolls, but if enrollment criteria were to change, as some Arapaho urge and others resist, additional enrollees are estimated to range from 600 to 3,000. A realistic figure for the total of the two branches probably lies between 7,000 and 8,000 Arapaho by self-definition, regardless of the degree of so-called Indian blood an individual may claim.

The history of the past century and a half has been anything but kind to the Arapaho, yet they have managed to persist and to survive as a distinct group. What does the future hold for them? In part this will depend on their ability and desire to maintain their ethnic consciousness and some elements of their ancient heritage; by the same token, the people of this country and the United States government have responsibility to see to it that those who were among the original keepers of this land are aided and encouraged by all means possible to keep alive the Arapaho version of what it is to be human.

Topically Indexed Bibliography of Sources Concerning the Arapaho Indians

Guide to Sources Concerning the Arapaho Indians

The purpose of this bibliographical essay is to guide the user of the topi-
cally indexed bibliography to the basic sources concerning the Arapaho Indians.
Works that have been singled out below are referred to by the last name of the
author and, parenthetically, the corresponding entry number of the bibliography.
In the main, published works have been given preference over unpublished theses or
dissertations, and secondary sources are listed only if including them is justified
by their scope. References to public documents of the United States have been excluded. Because the topical index appended to the bibliography makes it easy to
identify sources according to more than thirty different subject areas, the guide
is no more than the term implies.

Anthropologists will no doubt note with interest that a great deal of what we
know about the traditional culture of the Arapaho is due to the work of none other
than A. L. Kroeber who, with the encouragement of Franz Boas, made his first two
field trips to the Arapaho of Oklahoma and Wyoming in 1899 and 1900. Kroeber's
research among the two groups resulted in a number of important publications. The
decorative art and symbolism of the Arapaho, which was the subject of Kroeber's
doctoral dissertation, is dealt with in several works (308, 309, 311, and 312).
We are further indebted to Kroeber for a description of Arapaho ceremonial organization (313) and religion (314). Sources 312-314 have recently been reissued in
one volume (317). Together with Dorsey, Kroeber recorded nearly one hundred and
fifty traditional narratives, from both the Oklahoma and Wyoming branches of the
Arapaho (132); this collection remains the most complete source of Arapaho oral
folklore to date. In addition to the rich information on the Arapaho culture and
folklore that all these publications have furnished, Kroeber also added to our
knowledge of the Arapaho language (315), although the first significant contribution
to that subject was made by Hayden (256), dating back to the 1860s.

Kroeber's account of Arapaho religion was complemented by a detailed description by Dorsey of the sun dance ceremony as carried out by the Southern Arapaho
(Oklahoma) in 1901 and 1902 (130). Subsequently, a brief note on the sun dance
from the post-World War II period was published by Hultkrantz (279). The ceremony
of covering the Flat Pipe, the most sacred object of the Northern Arapaho, has been
described in some detail by Carter (78).

Structure of the Arapaho language received more systematic attention after
World War II by Salzmann (486, 491, 494-500, and 511), whose published data also
served as the basis for Goddard's outline of the historical phonology of Arapaho
and Atsina (Gros Ventre), its close relative (219). Structure of the Plains Indian
sign language, studied from data obtained primarily from a Northern Arapaho infor-
mant, is the subject of a doctoral dissertation by West (660).

The large body of Arapaho traditional narratives collected by Dorsey and
Kroeber has been expanded by Salzmann, who published some Arapaho tales in the
original language (487, 488, and in a slightly revised form as 502) and others as
told in English (483, 489, 503, 512, and 513). A further addition to the corpus
of Arapaho tales was made by Voth (644).

Arapaho music has received considerable attention over the past hundred years.
Mooney's collection of Arapaho ghost-dance songs from 1890 to 1894 (381) was followed by Densmore's monograph concerning Cheyenne and Arapaho music (125), several
articles by Nettl (especially 409, 412, 413, and 415), whose master's thesis dealt
with the musical culture of the Arapaho in general (408), and quite recently by
Lah's doctoral dissertation on Northern Arapaho music from an ethnoaesthetic point
of view (326).

An important source concerning Arapaho traditional culture is a study by Hilger (266) that, although concentrating on Arapaho child life, provides a wealth of general background data. Among the remaining contributions toward our understanding of the Arapaho are works focusing on kinship system and terminology by Eggan (142), Michelson (373), and Salzmann (490); social organization by Eggan (143) and Muntsch (399); the use of peyote in ceremonial context by Stenberg (587); and values by Gross (230-232) and Leacock (334). The acculturation of the Northern Arapaho is the subject of a study by Elkin (146), based on a doctoral dissertation. An overall view of the Arapaho people from the inside, but influenced by published sources, may be found in Shakespeare (533), a Northern Arapaho.

A comprehensive account of Northern Arapaho political history between 1851 and 1964 and modern tribal politics up to 1978 has been recently published by Fowler (190), who has also written on aspects of contemporary tribal economy (187 and 192) and political process (189 and 191). The latest anthropological study of the Northern Arapaho was made by Welsh (659), whose doctoral dissertation focuses on the contemporary and historical distribution of resources on the Wind River Reservation (Wyoming) and shows that while they have been struggling to retain sociopolitical independence, the Northern Arapaho are becoming increasingly dependent economically on the larger non-Indian society that surrounds them. How traditional concepts change in light of modern socioeconomic conditions is the subject of Hunter's master's thesis (285), based on data from the northern branch.

The history of modern education among the Southern Arapaho is the subject of a master's thesis by Sanders (514) and a doctoral dissertation by Whiteman (666). A study of the effect of modern education among the Northern Arapaho is the topic of Garcia's master's thesis (204).

Among available ethnohistorical studies, the broadest is a report (20) prepared in the 1950s for the Indian Claims Commission by several authors; it deals with the aboriginal land occupation of the Cheyenne and Arapaho (234), the historical development of their land area (240), and the relations between these two tribes and the United States (144). The history of the Southern Arapaho and their famous chief Left Hand has recently been published by Coel (95), while Trenholm has produced a volume dealing with the ethnohistory of both branches (622). More specifically, what the government policy and reservation and agency life were like for the Cheyenne and Arapaho of Oklahoma during the period 1875 to 1907 has been described by Berthrong (46, 48-50, 52, and 53), while Murphy has assessed the place of the Northern Arapaho in the relations between the United States and the Plains Indians during the period 1851 to 1879 (403).

Missionary activities among the Northern Arapaho are the subject of master's theses by Duncombe (135), focusing on St. Michael's Mission (Episcopal), and Henry (265), concerning St. Stephen's Indian Mission (Catholic). How modern Catholicism views traditional Arapaho religion and its Indian mission is discussed by Starkloff (578).

Introduction to the Bibliography

The purpose of this bibliography is to provide a comprehensive and reliable listing of sources concerning all aspects of the Arapaho people and their culture--in both the past and the present. The bibliography includes entries pertaining to the Northern (Wyoming) and Southern (Oklahoma) Arapaho, but not to the Atsina (Gros Ventre) of Montana, their close relative.

In addition to the published materials, the bibliography includes references to theses, dissertations, and several unpublished reports duplicated for distribution. The listing is complete for primary sources, and should be regarded as reasonably complete for secondary sources. Publications dealing with the Plains Indians in general have been omitted unless they include a significant amount of information about the Arapaho; to do otherwise would have enlarged the scope of the work beyond its intended purpose. Instead, the interested user is referred to the fourth edition (1975) of Ethnographic bibliography of North America, compiled by George Peter Murdock and Timothy J. O'Leary. With only a few exceptions, articles published in local and regional newspapers as well as reviews of works dealing with the Arapaho have been excluded.

The bibliographic entries are arranged alphabetically by author--or when no author is given, by title--and are numbered consecutively. The nature of each item's contents is briefly indicated by the abbreviations in brackets at the end of the entry. Abbreviations and the content categories to which they refer are listed below:

A	archaeology
B	bibliography
BE	business/economics
CA	contemporary affairs (post-WW II)
CC	culture change
CT	child training (traditional)
D	dance
DA	decorative art
EH	ethnohistory/history
F	fiction
FP	food preparation
G	games
H	health
IM	instructional material
IR	interethnic relations
K	kinship
L	language/linguistics
LH	life histories
M	music

MB   medicine/biology

MC   material culture (shelter, clothing, etc.)

ME   modern education

MG   miscellaneous and general information

NA   Northern Arapaho (primarily or exclusively)

OF   oral folklore

P   psychology

PD   pictorial documentation

PS   political/social organization

R   religion

RE   reservation ecology

S   subsistence

SA   Southern Arapaho (primarily or exclusively)

TL   treaties/legal affairs

V   values

A topical index referring to the numbered entries can be found following the bibliography on pp. 59-61.

Bibliography

1. Albaugh, Bernard J., and Philip O. Anderson. Peyote in the treatment of alcoholism among American Indians. The American Journal of Psychiatry 131:1247-1250 (1974). [CA, H, MB, R, SA]

2. Albert D. Richardson and Little Raven. The Trail 7:8:16-17 (January 1914). Denver, CO. [LH, PD]

3. Ambler, Marjane. Who controls the oil? Nations; The Native American Magazine 1:2:20-23 (August 1981). Seattle, WA. [BE, NA, PD, RE]

4. Ambler, Marjane. Nuclear homestead. Nations; The Native American Magazine 1:3:19-21 (September-October 1981). Seattle, WA. [CA, H, MB, NA, PD]

5. Ambler, Marjane. Wind River women; change in a traditional culture. Wyoming Horizons; Sunday Supplement to Casper Star-Tribune (January 1, 1984). Pp. 8-10. Casper, WY. [CC, NA, PD]

6. Ancient Arapaho invocation. The Wind River Rendezvous 11:6:[26] (November-December 1981). Saint Stephens, WY: Saint Stephens Indian Mission. [NA, R]

7. Anderson, A. M. Friday--the Arapaho Indian. (The American Adventure Series.) Chicago, IL: Wheeler Publishing Company, 1951. 172 pp. [F, IM, LH, MG, NA, PD]

8. Anderson, A. M. Teacher's guide book [for Friday--the Arapaho Indian. (The American Adventure Series.)]. Evanston, IL: Harper and Row, 1951, 1962. 32 pp. [F, IM, LH, MG, NA]

9. Anderson, Richard Tolbert. Federal relations with the Southern Cheyenne-Arapaho Indians, 1825-1869. M. A. thesis (History), University of Oklahoma. Norman, OK, 1962. iii + 137 pp. [EH, MG, SA, TL]

10. Anderson, William Marshall. The Rocky Mountain journals of William Marshall Anderson; the West in 1834. Ed. by Dale L. Morgan and Eleanor Towles Harris. San Marino, CA: The Huntington Library, 1967. 430 pp. [EH]

11. Andrist, Ralph K. The long death; the last days of the Plains Indian. New York, NY: The Macmillan Company, 1964. 371 pp. [CC, EH, IR, MG, PD, R, TL]

12. Antelope, Monica T. Clothing, shelter[s] [,] and transportation. Ethete, WY: Wyoming Indian High School, [1984]. 35 pp. [CC, DA, IM, MC, MG, NA, PD]

13. Arapaho. The Encyclopaedia Britannica; a Dictionary of Arts, Sciences, Literature and General Information, 11th edition. Vol. 2, Andros to Austria, p. 319. Cambridge [England]: at the University Press, 1910. [MG]

14. Arapaho. Encyclopaedia Britannica; a New Survey of Universal Knowledge. Vol. 2, Annual Register to Baltic Sea, p. 214. Chicago, IL: Encyclopaedia Britannica, 1929, 1949. [MG]

15. Arapaho. Great Soviet Encyclopedia. A translation of the third edition, 1970. Vol. 2, p. 232. New York, NY: Macmillan, 1973. [MG]

16. Arapaho. The New Encyclopaedia Britannica, Micropaedia. Vol. 1, Ǎ-Bib, pp. 477-478. Chicago, IL: Encyclopaedia Britannica, 1974. [MG]

17. Arapaho [2 traditional tales: Coyote loses his eyes and Coyote and the dwarf's arrow.] Saint Stephens, WY: Saint Stephens Indian School, 1979. [4 + 4 pp.] [IM, OF, PD]

18. Arapaho [2 traditional tales: Bear, the six brothers and the sister and Coyote and Whirlwind Woman.] Saint Stephens, WY: Saint Stephens Indian School, 1979. [4 + 4 pp.] [IM, OF, PD]

19. Arapaho & Shoshoni...and the buffalo. The Wind River Rendezvous 13:2:8 (April-June, 1983). Saint Stephens, WY: St. Stephen's Indian Mission Foundation. [NA, PD, S]

20. Arapaho-Cheyenne Indians. New York, NY: Garland Publishing, 1974. 342 pp. [EH, IR, MG, NA, SA, TL]

21. Arapaho Indians. The Encyclopedia Americana; International edition. Vol. 2, Ankara to Azusa, p. 170. Danbury, CT: Americana Corporation, 1980. [MG]

22. [Arapaho issue of] The Wind River Rendezvous 15:3:1-16 (July-September 1985). Saint Stephens, WY: St. Stephen's Indian Mission Foundation. [EH, MG, NA, PD]

23. Arapaho Mass--"Batan tawtini hinonoei." The Wind River Rendezvous 11:2:4-5 (March-April 1981). Saint Stephens, WY: Saint Stephens Indian Mission. [CC, NA, PD, R]

24. Arapaho naming-ceremony. The Wind River Rendezvous 5:3:4-5 (May-June 1975). Saint Stephens, WY: Saint Stephens Indian Mission. [L, NA]

25. Arapaho stories, legends and recollections. Ethete, WY: Wyoming Indian High School, 1979. [71 pp.] [EH, IM, MC, MG, NA, OF, PD]

26. The Arapahoe Indians. The Trail 7:4:20-23 (September 1914). Denver, CO. [EH, MG]

27. Arapahos in early Denver. The Wind River Rendezvous 11:1:7-9 (January-February 1981). Saint Stephens, WY: Saint Stephens Indian Mission. [EH, NA, PD]

28. Armstrong, Robert Gelston. The acculturation of the Cheyenne and Arapaho Indians. M.A. thesis (Anthropology), University of Oklahoma. Norman, OK, 1942. iv + 131 pp. [CC, EH, IR, MC, MG, R, RE, SA]

29. Arps, Louisa Ward, and Elinor Eppich Kingery. High country names; Rocky Mountain National Park. Denver, CO: The Colorado Mountain Club, 1966. 212 pp. [EH, MG, PD]

30. Arthur, Fremont (Jaitdahait). Questions and answers in Arapahoe. Nunaae nodawa nau hauchaneheet. [n.d.] 20 pp. [L, R]

31. As the world turns. The Wind River Rendezvous 5:1:6-7 (January-February 1975). Saint Stephens, WY: Saint Stephens Indian Mission. [LH, MG, NA]

32. Athearn, Robert G. Colorado and the Indian War of 1868. The Colorado Magazine 33:42-51 (1956). Denver, CO. [EH]

33. Bachman, Dona. A guide to the Plains Indian Gallery for young people. Cheyenne, WY: [Wyoming] State Museum Volunteers, 1985. 28 pp. [IM, L, MG, NA, PD]

34. Baker, John L. An economic analysis of alternatives for the use of agricultural resources on the Wind River Reservation, Wyoming. M.S. thesis (Agricultural Economics), University of Wyoming. Laramie, WY, 1960. vi + 100 pp. [BE, CA, CC, NA, RE]

35. Balcom, Royal H. St. Michael's Mission for Arapahoes [sic] Indians in Wyoming. The Southern Workman 48:441-447 (1919). [CC, ME, NA, PD, R]

36. [Balcom, Royal H.] St. Michael's Mission project at Ethete, Wyoming. [1924?]
     12 pp. [BE, CC, NA, R]

37. Bancroft, Hubert Howe. The works of Hubert Howe Bancroft. Volume XXV: History
     of Nevada, Colorado, and Wyoming, 1540-1888. San Francisco, CA: The History
     Company, 1890. [EH, IR, NA, TL]

38. Barry, Lawrence E. The Indian in a cultural trap. America (National Catholic
     Weekly Review) 112:482-484 (April 10, 1965) [No. 2910]. [CA, CC, MG, NA]

39. Bass, Althea. Carl Sweezy, Arapaho artist. The Chronicles of Oklahoma 34:429-
     431 (1956). [LH, PD, SA]

40. Bass, Althea. The Arapaho way; a memoir of an Indian boyhood. New York, NY:
     Clarkson N. Potter, 1966. xx + 80 pp. [CC, IR, LH, MG, PD, R, SA]

41. Battey, Thomas C. The life and adventures of a Quaker among the Indians.
     Boston, MA: Lee and Shepard, Publishers, [1875] 1876. [MG, SA]

42. Beals, Ralph L. Ethnology of Rocky Mountain Park: the Ute and Arapaho. Berke-
     ley, CA: U.S. Department of the Interior, National Park Service, Field Divis-
     ion of Education, 1936. [iii +] 27 pp. [DA, MC, MG, NA, PS, R, S]

43. Bell, John R. The journal of Captain John R. Bell, official journalist for the
     Stephen H. Long expedition to the Rocky Mountains, 1820. Ed. and introduced
     by Harlin M. Fuller and LeRoy R. Hafen. Glendale, CA: The Arthur H. Clark
     Company, 1957. 349 pp. [MG]

44. Bender, Jessie Fremont. The Cheyenne and Arapaho Indians, 1861-1892. M.A.
     thesis (History), University of Oklahoma. Norman, OK, 1930. i + 211 pp.
     [EH, MG, SA]

45. Benedict, Ruth Fulton. The vision in Plains culture. American Anthropologist
     24:1-23 (1922). [R]

46. Berthrong, Donald J. Federal Indian policy and the Southern Cheyennes and
     Arapahoes, 1887-1907. Ethnohistory 3:138-153 (1956). [EH, IR, SA, TL]

47. Berthrong, Donald J. The Southern Cheyennes. Norman, OK: University of Okla-
     homa Press, 1963. xiv + 442 pp. [EH, MG, PD, SA, TL]

48. Berthrong, Donald J. Cattlemen on the Cheyenne-Arapaho reservation, 1883-1885.
     Arizona and the West 13:5-32 (1971). [CC, EH, IR, RE, SA]

49. Berthrong, Donald J. White neighbors come among the Southern Cheyenne and
     Arapaho. Kansas Quarterly 3:4:105-115 (1971). [CC, EH, SA]

50. Berthrong, Donald J. Federal Indian policy and the Southern Cheyennes and
     Arapahoes, 1887-1907. In The Western American Indian: case studies in tribal
     history. Richard N. Ellis, ed. Pp. 133-143. Lincoln, NE: University of
     Nebraska Press, 1972. [CC, EH, TL]

51. Berthrong, Donald J. Review of Virginia Cole Trenholm, The Arapahoes, our
     people. Pacific Historical Review 41:242-243 (1972).

52. Berthrong, Donald J. The Cheyenne and Arapaho ordeal; reservation and agency
     life in the Indian Territory, 1875-1907. (The Civilization of the American
     Indian Series, Vol. 136.) Norman, OK: University of Oklahoma Press, 1976.
     xv + 402 pp. [CC, EH, IR, PD, RE, SA]

53. Berthrong, Donald J. Legacies of the Dawes Act: bureaucrats and land thieves
     at the Cheyenne-Arapaho agencies of Oklahoma. In The Plains Indians of the
     twentieth century. Peter Iverson, ed. Pp. 31-53. Norman, OK: University of
     Oklahoma Press, 1985. [BE, EH, PD, SA, TL]

54. Bierhorst, John, ed. The red swan; myths and tales of the American Indians.
     New York, NY: Farrar, Straus and Giroux, 1976. [viii +] 386 pp. [OF]

55. Bierhorst, John. The mythology of North America. New York, NY: William Morrow and Company, 1985. ix + 259 pp. [OF]

56. Blackmore, William. The North-American Indians: a sketch of some of the hostile tribes, together with a brief account of General Sheridan's campaign of 1868 against the Sioux, Cheyenne, Arapahoe, Kiowa, and Comanche Indians. The Journal of the Ethnological Society of London 1(n.s.):287-320 (1869). [EH, IR, MG, TL]

57. Blumensohn, Jules. The fast among North American Indians. American Anthropologist 35:451-469 (1933). [R]

58. Boas, Franz. Zur Anthropologie der nordamerikanischen Indianer. Zeitschrift für Ethnologie 27:366-411 (1895). Berlin. [MB]

59. Boas, Franz. Primitive art. New York, NY: Dover Publications, 1955. [1st ed. in 1927] [DA, PD]

60. Bolton, Herbert E. New light on Manuel Lisa and the Spanish fur trade. The Southwestern Historical Quarterly 17:61-66 (1913-1914). [EH]

61. Bourke, John G. On the border with Crook. New York, NY: Charles Scribner's Sons, 1892. Glorieta, NM: The Rio Grande Press, 1969. xiii + 508 pp. [EH, MG, PD]

62. Boyd, Evelyn J., and Bob Spoonhunter. Arts and crafts; student handbook. Ethete, WY: Wyoming Indian High School, 1982. 29 pp. [DA, IM, MC, PD]

63. Boyer, Warren E. The thunder bird. Sunset 60:6:19 (June 1928). [R]

64. Brady, G. M. The story of Little Silver Hair. Manuscripts 28:292-299 (1976). [EH, NA]

65. Brenton, John K. Study into the effects of per capita payments made to Arapahoe and Shoshone of the Wind River Reservation, May 1947-March 1950. 1950. 11 + 2 [+ ii]. [Typescript.] [BE, NA, S]

66. Buckles, William G. Archaeology in Colorado: historic tribes. Southwestern Lore 34:53-67 (1968). [EH, MG, PD]

67. Buntin, Martha. Difficulties encountered in issuing Cheyenne and Arapaho subsistence, 1861-1870. Chronicles of Oklahoma 13:37-45 (1935). [EH, S, SA]

68. Buschmann, Joh. Carl Ed. Die Spuren der aztekischen Sprache im nördlichen Mexico und höheren amerikanischen Norden. Zugleich eine Musterung der Völker und Sprachen des nördlichen Mexico's und der Westseite Nordamerika's von Guadalaxara an bis zum Eismeer. Abhandlungen der Königlichen Akademie der Wissenschaften zu Berlin. Aus dem Jahre 1854. 2nd suppl. vol. 1859. [EH, L]

69. Bushnell, David I., Jr. Villages of the Algonquian, Siouan, and Caddoan tribes west of the Mississippi. Smithsonian Institution, Bureau of American Ethnology, Bulletin 77. [Arapaho, pp. 33-37]. Washington, DC: GPO, 1922. [EH, MG, PD]

70. Butler, Helen. A stone upon his shoulder. Philadelphia, PA: The Westminster Press, 1953. 272 pp. [F, NA]

71. Byron, Elsa Spear. The Fetterman fight. Annals of Wyoming 36:63-66 (1964). [EH, NA]

72. Callahan, Charles J. Historical sketch of Two Babies, Arapaho Indian. The Chronicles of Oklahoma 45:217-220 (1967). [IR, LH, PD, SA]

73. Campbell, John. Origin of the aborigines of Canada. Transactions of the Literary and Historical Society of Quebec, Sessions of 1880-81. Pp. 61-93, i-xxxiv. Quebec, 1880. [L]

74. Campbell, John. Affiliation of the Algonquin languages. Proceedings of the Canadian Institute 1(n.s.):15-53 (1884). Toronto. [L]

75. Canton, Frank M. Frontier trails; the autobiography of Frank M. Canton. Ed. by Edward Everett Dale. Norman, OK: University of Oklahoma Press, 1930, 1966. xix + 237 pp. [EH, NA]

76. Cardinal, Barbara. Mike learns about....Saint Stephens, WY: Saint Stephens Indian School, 1977. 13 pp. [H, L, NA]

77. Carriker, Robert Charles. Fort Supply, Indian Territory: frontier outpost on the southern Plains, 1868-1894. Dissertation Abstracts: The Humanities and Social Sciences 28:6:2158-A (December 1967). [EH, IR]

78. Carter, John G. The Northern Arapaho Flat Pipe and the ceremony of covering the pipe. Smithsonian Institution, Bureau of American Ethnology, Bulletin 119 (Anthropological Papers, No. 2), pp. 71-102. Washington, DC: GPO, 1938. [NA, PD, R]

79. Carter, Joseph LeRoy. Dian takes to the Indians. 1979. 105 pp. [EH, R, SA]

80. Cedartree, Helen. Wind River memories. Ethete, WY: Wyoming Indian High School, 1984. 24 pp. [BE, EH, LH, ME, MG, NA, PD, RE]

81. Celebrations. The Wind River Rendezvous 15:1:3-12 (January-March 1985). Saint Stephens, WY: St. Stephen's Indian Mission Foundation. [CA, NA, PD, R]

82. [Chamberlain, Alexander Francis and Isabel C.]. Record of American folk-lore. [Review of George A. Dorsey, The Arapaho sun dance; the ceremony of the offerings lodge.] The Journal of American Folk-Lore 17:61-76 (1904).

83. Cheyenne and Arapahoe troubles. The United States Army and Navy Journal, and Gazette of the Regular and Volunteer Forces. Vol. XXIII, No. 2 (Whole No. 1146), p. 24. New York, August 8, 1885. [EH, SA]

84. Chittenden, Hiram Martin. The American fur trade of the Far West. Vol. 2, pp. 483-1014. New York, NY: Barnes and Noble, 1935. [MG]

85. Clark, Ella E. Indian legends from the northern Rockies. Norman, OK: University of Oklahoma Press, 1966. xxv + 350 pp. [OF]

86. Clark, W. P. The Indian sign language, with brief explanatory notes of the gestures taught deaf-mutes in our institutions for their instruction, and a description of some of the peculiar laws, customs, myths, superstitions, ways of living, code of peace and war signals of our aborigines. Philadelphia, PA: L. R. Hamersly and Co., 1885. [L, MG]

87. Clark, W. P. The Indian sign language. Lincoln, NE: University of Nebraska Press, 1982. 443 pp. [L, MG]

88. Cockerham, William C. Drinking attitudes and practices among Wind River Reservation Indian youth. Journal of Studies on Alcohol 36:321-326 (1975). [CA, H, NA]

89. Cockerham, William C., and Morris A. Forslund. Attitudes toward the police among white and Native American youth. American Indian Law Review 3:419-428 (1975). [CA, IR, NA, TL, V]

90. Cockerham, William C., and Morris A. Forslund. Attitudes toward the police among white and Native American youth. In Social research for consumers. By Earl R. Babbie. Pp. 355-363. Belmont, CA: Wadsworth Publishing Company, 1982. [CA, IR, NA, TL, V]

91. Cockerham, William C., Morris A. Forslund, and Rolland M. Raboin. Drug use among white and American Indian high school youth. The International Journal of the Addictions 11:209-220 (1976). [CA, H, NA]

92. Cocking, Rodney R. A cultural exploration of fantasy confession: the Arapaho
     Indian. M.A. thesis (Psychology, University of Wyoming. Laramie, WY, 1966.
     ix + 124 pp. [NA, P]

93. Cocking, Rodney R. Fantasy confession among Arapaho Indian children. The
     Journal of Genetic Psychology 114:229-235 (1969). [NA, P]

94. Coe, Ralph T. Sacred circles; two thousand years of North American Indian art.
     London: Arts Council of Great Britain, 1976. 236 pp. [DA, MC, PD]

95. Coel, Margaret. Chief Left Hand, Southern Arapaho. (The Civilization of the
     American Indian Series, Vol. 159.) Norman, OK: University of Oklahoma Press,
     1981. xiv + 338 pp. [EH, IR, LH, MG, PD, SA]

96. Cohen, Felix S. Handbook of federal Indian law. Albuquerque, NM: University
     of New Mexico Press, [1942, n.d.]. xxxviii + 662 pp. [TL]

97. Collings, Ellsworth. Roman Nose: chief of the Southern Cheyenne. The Chroni-
     cles of Oklahoma 42:429-457 (1964). [EH, IR, SA]

98. Collins, Hubert E. Warpath & cattle trail. New York, NY: William Morrow &
     Company, 1928, 1933. xix + 296 pp. [EH, IR, SA]

99. Commission findings. In Arapaho-Cheyenne Indians. Pp. 227-342. New York, NY:
     Garland Publishing, 1974. [EH, TL]

100. Constitution and bylaws of the Arapahoe tribe of Indians, Wind River Indian
      Reservation, State of Wyoming. [1949?] 5 + 2 pp. [CA, NA, PS, TL]

101. Constitution and by-laws of the Cheyenne-Arapaho tribes of Oklahoma. Ratified
      September 18, 1937.—Amendments to Constitution and by-laws of the Cheyenne-
      Arapaho tribes of Oklahoma. Washington, DC: GPO, 1938. 5 + 2 pp. [CA, PS,
      SA, TL]

102. Coolidge, Grace. Two Indian stories. The Outlook 100:651-655 (March 23, 1912).
      [F]

103. Coolidge, Grace. The nothing gift—tepee neighbors. Collier's 51:23:17, 34
      (August 23, 1913). [F, NA]

104. Coolidge, Grace. The victory. Collier's 51:25:16-17 (September 6, 1913).
      [F, NA]

105. Coolidge, Grace. Place of thanksgiving. Collier's 52:2:17 (September 27,
      1913). [F]

106. Coolidge, Grace. Teepee neighbors. Boston, MA: The Four Seas Company, 1917.
      225 pp. [F, NA]

107. Coolidge, Grace. Teepee neighbors. Norman, OK: University of Oklahoma Press,
      1984. xxxv + 163 pp. [F, NA]

108. Coolidge, Sherman. The Indian American—his duty to his race and to his coun-
      try, The United States of America. The Quarterly Journal of the Society of
      American Indians 1:1:20-24 (1913). Washington, DC. [MG]

109. Coolidge, Sherman. The American Indian of today. The Quarterly Journal of
      the Society of American Indians 2:1:33-35 (1914). Washington, DC. [MG]

110. Cooper, Baird S. Wind River reservation[,] Wyoming. Hartford, CT: Church
      Missions Publishing Company, [n.d.]. 18 pp. [CC, LH, MG, NA, OF, PD, R]

111. Cornett, Lloyd H. Leasing and utilization of land of the Cheyenne and
      Arapaho Indians, 1891-1907. M. A. thesis (History), University of Oklahoma.
      Norman, OK, 1954. xvi + 284 pp. [CC, RE, SA, TL]

112. Cranston, Virginia A. Indian and white delinquency: a self-report study
     of Wyoming youth. M.A. thesis (Sociology), University of Wyoming. Laramie,
     WY, 1975. iv + 100 pp. [CA, IR, MG, NA, P, V]

113. Crispin, Tom. The four old men [by Tom Crispin, Arapaho, as told to Mary
     Heaton Vorse]. Indians at Work 2:20:12-13 (June 1, 1935). Washington, DC:
     Office of Indian Affairs. [NA, OF]

114. Culin, Stewart. A summer trip among the western Indians. (The Wanamaker Ex-
     pedition). Bulletin of the Free Museum of Science and Art of the University
     of Pennsylvania 3:1:1-22 (1901). Philadelphia, PA. [MC, NA, PD]

115. Culin, Stewart. Games of the North American Indians. Twenty-fourth Annual
     Report of the Bureau of American Ethnology to the Secretary of the Smith-
     sonian Institution, 1902-1903. Pp. 3-846. Washington, DC: GPO, 1907.
     [G, MC, PD]

116. Curtis, Edward S. The North American Indian; being a series of volumes pictur-
     ing and describing the Indians of the United States and Alaska. Vol. 6,
     pp. 137-150, 159-173. Cambridge, MA, 1911. [L, M, MG, PD]

117. Curtis, Natalie. The Indians' book; an offering by the American Indians of
     Indian lore, musical and narrative, to form a record of the songs and legends
     of their race. New York, NY: Harper and Brothers, 1907. Pp. 195-217, 545-
     546. [L, M]

118. Custer, George A. My life on the Plains. Chicago, IL: The Lakeside Press,
     1952. Lincoln, NE: University of Nebraska Press, 1966. xlii + 626 pp.
     [EH, IR, PD, TL]

119. Dale, Edward Everett. Ranching on the Cheyenne-Arapaho reservation 1880-1885.
     The Chronicles of Oklahoma 6:35-59 (1928). [EH, IR, RE, SA, TL]

120. Dale, Edward Everett. The Cheyenne-Arapaho country. The Chronicles of Okla-
     homa 20:360-371 (1942). [BE, EH, RE, SA]

121. Dangberg, Grace M., ed. Letters to Jack Wilson, the Paiute prophet, written
     between 1908 and 1911. Smithsonian Institution, Bureau of American Ethnolo-
     gy, Bulletin 164 (Anthropological papers, No. 55), pp. 279-296. Washington,
     DC: GPO, 1957. [EH, NA, R]

122. David, Robert Beebe. Finn Burnett[,] frontiersman; the life and adventures of
     an Indian fighter, mail coach driver, miner, pioneer cattleman, participant
     in the Powder River expedition, survivor of the Hay Field fight, associate
     of Jim Bridger and Chief Washakie. Glendale, CA: The Arthur H. Clark Com-
     pany, 1937. 378 pp. [EH, NA]

123. Delisle, Gilles L. On the so-called fourth person in Algonquian. Working
     Papers on Language Universals, No. 12, pp. 69-83 (November 1973). [L]

124. Densmore, Frances. A study of Cheyenne and Arapaho music. The Masterkey
     9:187-189 (1935). [M, SA]

125. Densmore, Frances. Cheyenne and Arapaho music. Southwest Museum Papers,
     No. 10. Los Angeles, CA: Southwest Museum, 1936. 111 pp. [D, M, PD, R, SA]

126. Dictionary of Indian tribes of the Americas. Vol. 1, pp. 134-142. Newport
     Beach, CA: American Indian Publishers, 1980. [MG]

127. Dobler, Lavinia. Wild wind, wild water. Casper, WY: Misty Mountain Press,
     1983. [iii +] 259 pp. [EH, MG, NA]

128. Dodge, Richard Irving. Our wild Indians: thirty-three years' personal experi-
     ence among the red men of the great West. A popular account of their social
     life, religion, habits, traits, customs, exploits, etc. with thrilling adven-
     tures and experiences on the Great Plains and in the mountains of our wide
     frontier. Hartford, CT, 1890. [IR, MG, SA]

129. Domenech, Abbé Em.[anuel Henri]. Seven years' residence in the great deserts of North America. Vol. 2. London, 1860. [L]

130. Dorsey, George A. The Arapaho sun dance; the ceremony of the offerings lodge. Field Columbian Museum, Publication 75, Anthropological Series, Vol. 4. Chicago, IL: Field Columbian Museum, 1903. xii + 228 pp. [D, DA, L, OF, PD, PS, R, SA]

131. Dorsey, George A. The Arapaho. Unfinished MS, [1905]. ii + 212 pp. [MC]

132. Dorsey, George A., and Alfred L. Kroeber. Traditions of the Arapaho. Field Columbian Museum, Publication 81, Anthropological Series, Vol. 5. Chicago, IL: Field Columbian Museum, 1903. x + 475 pp. [L, OF]

133. Douglas, Frederic H. A Northern Arapaho quilled cradle. Denver Art Museum, Material Culture Notes, No. 13, pp. 53-60. Denver, CO: Denver Art Museum, Department of Indian Art, 1941. [DA, MC, NA, PD]

134. Duncan, W[alter] A[dair], Rev. Claim of Cheyennes and Arapahoes to certain Cherokee lands, considered in the light of facts. Tahlequah, C.N. [Cherokee Nation], 1889. 23 pp. [EH, SA, TL]

135. Duncombe, Edward S. Ethete: Episcopal churchwork among the Northern Arapahoes, 1883-1925. M.A. thesis (American Studies), University of Wyoming. Laramie, WY, 1981. x + 100 pp. [CC, MG, NA, R]

136. Duncombe, Patricia. Within the Circle. Cincinnati, OH: Forward Movement Publications, 1981. 57 pp. [MG, NA, R, V]

137. Dunn, J. P. Massacres of the mountains: a history of the Indian Wars of the Far West, 1815-1875. New York, NY: Archer House, 1958. viii + 669 pp. [Chapter XIII.] [EH, NA, PD]

138. Dunnells, L. H. Indian life in Colorado; a collection of source material. M.A. thesis (History and Political Science), Colorado State College of Education. Greeley, CO, 1938. viii + 125 pp. [MG]

139. Durosko, Joyce Agnes. True Indian education: a viable future from a memory of the past. Specialist in Education thesis, University of Michigan. Ann Arbor, MI, 1980. vi + 127 pp. [EH, ME, MG, NA]

140. Dyer, D. B. (Mrs.). "Fort Reno" or picturesque "Cheyenne and Arrapahoe army life," before the opening of "Oklahoma." New York, NY: G. W. Dillingham, 1896. [EH, MG, SA]

141. The economy of the Wind River Indian Reservation, Wyoming (A summary report). U.S. Department of Agriculture, Soil Conservation Service, Technical Cooperation--Bureau of Indian Affairs. Denver, CO, 1938. 14 pp. [Mimeographed.] [BE, NA, RE]

142. Eggan Fred. The Cheyenne and Arapaho kinship system. In Social anthropology of North American tribes; essays in social organization, law, and religion. Fred Eggan, ed. Pp. 35-95. Chicago, IL: The University of Chicago Press, 1937. [K, L, PS, SA]

143. Eggan, Fred. The Cheyenne and Arapaho in the perspective of the Plains: ecology and society. In The American Indian: perspectives for the study of social change. By Fred Eggan. Pp. 45-77. Chicago, IL: Aldine Publishing Company, 1966. [MG, SA]

144. Ekirch, Arthur A. Historical background. In Arapaho-Cheyenne Indians. Pp. 175-225. New York, NY: Garland Publishing, 1974. [EH, IR, SA, TL]

145. Elkin, Henry. The Northern Arapaho of Wyoming. Ph.D. dissertation (Anthropology), Columbia University. New York, NY, 1940. [CC, IR, MG, NA]

146. Elkin, Henry. The Northern Arapaho of Wyoming. In Acculturation in seven
      American Indian tribes. Ralph Linton, ed. Pp. 207-258. New York, NY:
      D. Appleton-Century Company, 1940. [CC, IR, MG, NA]

147. Encyclopedia of Indians of the Americas. Vol. 2, pp. 203-207. St. Clair
      Shores, MI: Scholarly Press, 1974. [MG]

148. Erickson, Phoebe. Wildwing. New York, NY: Harper & Brothers, 1959. x +
      180 pp. [F]

149. Essin, Emmett M., III. The Southern Cheyennes. In Forked tongues and broken
      treaties. Donald E. Worcester, ed. Pp. 110-162. Caldwell, ID: The Caxton
      Printers, 1975. [EH, PD, SA, TL]

150. Ewers, John Canfield. Plains Indian painting; a description of an aboriginal
      American art. Stanford, CA: Stanford University Press, 1939. xiv + 84 pp.
      [DA, MC, PD]

151. Ewers, John C. Arapaho Indians. The World Book Encyclopedia, Vol. 1, A,
      p(p.) 551(-552). Chicago, IL, 1967, 1977. [MG]

152. Ewers, John C. Plains Indian sculpture; a traditional art from America's
      heartland. Washington, DC: Smithsonian Institution Press, 1986. 239 pp.
      [DA, MC, PD]

153. Eyster, Ira, project dir. Culture through concepts—a teachers guide [pp. 82-
      126]. Norman, OK: Southwest Center for Human Relations Study (University of
      Oklahoma), [1978]. 234 pp. [IM, LH, MG, PD, SA]

154. Eyster, Ira, project dir. Clues from the past. Norman, OK: Southwest Center
      for Human Relations Study (University of Oklahoma), 1981. 15 pp. [IM, MC,
      MG, PD, SA]

155. Eyster, Ira, project dir. Games and lessons. Norman, OK: Southwest Center
      for Human Relations Study (University of Oklahoma), 1981. 13 pp. [IM, MC,
      MG, PD, SA]

156. Eyster, Ira, project dir. Images. Norman, OK: Southwest Center for Human
      Relations Study (University of Oklahoma), 1981. 15 pp. [IM, MC, MG, PD, SA]

157. Eyster, Ira, project dir. People of the spirit. Norman, OK: Southwest Center
      for Human Relations Study (University of Oklahoma), 1981. 11 pp. [IM, MC,
      MG, PD, R, SA]

158. Eyster, Ira, project dir. Woodlands to Plains. Norman, OK: Southwest Center
      for Human Relations Study (University of Oklahoma), 1981. 15 pp. [IM, MC,
      MG, PD, SA]

159. Fairbanks, Robert A. The Cheyenne-Arapaho and alcoholism: does the tribe have
      a legal right to a medical remedy? American Indian Law Review 1:55-77 (1973).
      [H, SA, TL]

160. Farnham, Thomas J. Travels in the great Western prairies, the Anahuac and
      Rocky Mountains, and in the Oregon Territory. 2 vols. In Early Western
      travels, 1748-1846. Edited by Reuben Gold Thwaites. Vol. 28. Cleveland, OH:
      The Arthur H. Clark Company, [1843], 1906. 380 pp. [MG]

161. Fay, George E., ed. Constitution and by-laws of the Cheyenne-Arapaho tribes
      of Oklahoma. Ratified September 18, 1937. In Charters, constitutions and
      by-laws of the Indian tribes of North America, Part V: The Indian tribes of
      Oklahoma. Occasional Publications in Anthropology, Ethnology Series, No. 6,
      pp. 33-38. Greeley, CO: Museum of Anthropology, Colorado State College,
      1968. [PS, SA, TL]

162. Fay, George E., ed. Military engagements between United States troops and
      Plains Indians; documentary inquiry by the U.S. Congress. Occasional Publi-
      cations in Anthropology, Ethnology Series, No. 26, Part Ia: 1854-1867.
      Greeley, CO: Museum of Anthropology, University of Northern Colorado, 1972.
      iv + 116 pp. [EH, NA, TL]

163. Fay, George E., ed. Military engagements between United States troops and
      Plains Indians; documentary inquiry by the U.S. Congress. Occasional Pub-
      lications in Anthropology, Ethnology Series, No. 26, Part Ib: 1854-1867.
      Greeley, CO: Museum of Anthropology, University of Northern Colorado, 1972.
      iv + 117-236 pp. [EH, NA, TL]

164. Fay, George E., ed. Resolution of the legislature of Kansas,...in relation
      to outrages perpetrated by Sioux and Arapaho Indians in that state. Occasional
      Publications in Anthropology, Ethnology Series, No. 29: Military engagements
      between United States troops and Plains Indians, Part IV: 1872-1890. P. 1.
      Greeley, CO: Museum of Anthropology, University of Northern Colorado, 1973.
      [EH, TL]

165. Fay, George E., ed. Treaties, land cessions, and other U.S. Congressional
      documents relative to American Indian tribes. Treaties between the tribes
      of the Great Plains and the United States of America: Cheyenne and Arapaho,
      1825-1900, &c. Occasional Publications in Anthropology, Ethnology Series,
      No. 22. Greeley, CO: Museum of Anthropology, University of Northern Colo-
      rado, 1977. vi + 125 pp. [EH, TL]

166. Felde, Max [Johann Kaltenboeck]. Der Arrapahu; Erzählung aus der Zeit der
      Indianerkriege. Stuttgart: Union Deutsche Verlagsgesellschaft, [1900?],
      1939. 295 pp. [F]

167. Fifty-fourth Congress, first session; document No. 247. Annals of Wyoming
      8:528-539 (1931). [EH, NA, PD, TL]

168. Fisher, Morton C. On the Arapahoes, Kiowas, and Comanches. The Journal of
      the Ethnological Society of London 1(n.s.):274-287. London, 1869. [MG]

169. Fletcher, Alice C. Indian story and song from North America. Pp. 96-100.
      Boston, MA: Small Maynard and Company, 1900. [M]

170. Fletcher, Alice C. Review of George A. Dorsey, The Arapaho sun dance; the
      ceremony of the offerings lodge. American Anthropologist 6:156-160 (1904).

171. Foreman, Grant. The last trek of the Indians. Chicago, IL: The University of
      Chicago Press, 1946. 382 pp. [EH, MG]

172. Forslund, Morris A. Planning project in juvenile delinquency; prevention and
      control of delinquency among Indian youth in Wyoming. Laramie, WY: Univer-
      sity of Wyoming, 1972. vii + 78 pp. [Mimeographed.] [CA, NA, V]

173. Forslund, Morris A. Dependency/neglect and custody/guardianship cases among
      Wind River Indian Reservation youth: suggestions for needed research.
      Laramie, WY: University of Wyoming, 1973. 6 pp. [Mimeographed.] [K, NA, PS]

174. Forslund, Morris A. Data book I: Delinquency involvement among Lander Valley
      and Wind River high school students. Laramie, WY: University of Wyoming,
      1973. [ii +] 58 pp. [Mimeographed.] [CA, IR, NA, V]

175. Forslund, Morris A. Data book II: A comparison of Indian and non-Indian de-
      linquency in Wyoming. Laramie, WY: University of Wyoming, 1973. [i +]
      89 pp. [Mimeographed.] [CA, IR, NA, V]

176. Forslund, Morris A. Indian and non-Indian delinquency: a self report study of
      Wind River Reservation area youth. Laramie, WY: Department of Sociology,
      University of Wyoming, 1974. 57 pp. [CA, H, NA]

177. Forslund, Morris A. Data book III: Drug use and delinquency. Laramie, WY:
      University of Wyoming, 1974. [ii +] 45 pp. [Mimeographed.] [CA, IR, NA, V]

178. Forslund, Morris A. Indian juvenile delinquency—how different [?]. Laramie, WY: University of Wyoming, 1975. 7 pp. [Mimeographed.] [CA, NA, V]

179. Forslund, Morris A. Functions of drinking for Native American and white youth. Journal of Youth and Adolescence 7:327:332 (1978). [CA, H, MB, NA, V]

180. Forslund, Morris A. Drinking problems of Native American and white youth. Journal of Drug Education 9:1:21-27 (1979). [CA, H, MB, NA]

181. Forslund, Morris A., William C. Cockerham, and Rolland M. Raboin. Drug use, delinquency and alcohol use among Indian and Anglo youth in Wyoming. Laramie, WY: University of Wyoming, 1974. [i +] 61 pp. [Mimeographed.] [CA, IR, NA, V]

182. Forslund, Morris A., and Virginia Cranston. A self-report comparison of Indian and Anglo delinquency in Wyoming. Criminology 13:193-197 (1975). [CA, IR, NA, P, V]

183. Forslund, Morris A., and Ralph E. Meyers. Delinquency among Wind River Indian Reservation youth. Criminology 12:97-106 (1974). [Reprinted in American Indian Law Review 2:61-69.] [CA, H, NA, P]

184. Forslund, Morris A., and Betty L. Wells. Data book: Political socialization: Wind River Reservation area youth [,] grades five through eight. Laramie, WY: University of Wyoming, 1974. [1+] 314 pp. [Mimeographed.] [CA, IR, NA, V]

185. Forslund, Morris A., and Betty L. Wells. Political learning among members of a racial-ethnic minority. American Indian Culture and Research Journal 3:2:1-22 (1979). [CA, ME, NA, P]

186. Fowler, Loretta Kay. Political process and socio-cultural change among the Arapahoe Indians. Ph.D. dissertation (Anthropology), University of Illinois at Urbana-Champaign, IL, 1970. iv + 361 pp. [CA, CC, NA, PS]

187. Fowler, Loretta. The Arapahoe Ranch: an experiment in cultural change and economic development. Economic Development and Cultural Change 21:446-464 (1973). [BE, CA, CC, NA, RE]

188. Fowler, Loretta. Oral historian or ethnologist?: the career of Bill Shakespeare; Northern Arapaho, 1901-1975. In American Indian intellectuals. Margot Liberty, ed. 1976 Proceedings of the American Ethnological Society. Pp. 226-240. St. Paul, MN: West Publishing Company, 1978. [CA, CC, LH, NA, PD]

189. Fowler, Loretta. Wind River Reservation political process: an analysis of the symbols of consensus. American Ethnologist 5:748-769 (1978). [BE, CA, NA, PS, TL]

190. Fowler, Loretta. Arapahoe politics, 1851-1978; symbols in crises of authority. Lincoln, NE: University of Nebraska Press, 1982. xx + 373 pp. [BE, CA, CC, EH, IR, LH, MG, NA, PD, PS]

191. Fowler, Loretta. "Look at my hair, it is gray"; age grading, ritual authority, and political change among the Northern Arapahoes and Gros Ventres. In Plains Indian studies: a collection of essays in honor of John C. Ewers and Waldo R. Wedel. Douglas H. Ubelaker and Herman J. Viola, eds. Smithsonian Contributions to Anthropology, No. 30, pp. 73-93. Washington, DC: GPO, 1982. [CC, EH, IR, NA, PS, S]

192. Fowler, Loretta. "What they issue you": political economy at Wind River. In The Plains Indians of the twentieth century. Peter Iverson, ed. Pp. 187-217. Norman, OK: University of Oklahoma Press, 1985. [BE, IR, NA, PD, PS]

193. Freer, William B. The Southern Cheyenne and Arapaho fair. The Red Man 4:221-227 (1912). [MG, SA]

194. Friday, Ben, Sr. The story of Friday (Sitting in the Meek). William J.
      C'Hair, ed. and trans. Ethete, WY: Wyoming Indian High School, [n.d.].
      [11 pp.] [IM, LH, NA, PD]

195. Friday, Ben, Sr. Sleeping Boy. William J. C'Hair, ed. and trans. Ethete, WY:
      Wyoming Indian High School, [n.d.]. [10 pp.] [OF, PD]

196. Friday, Moses. Arapaho tradition of creation. The Carlisle Arrow 7:2:1 (Sep-
      tember 16, 1910). Carlisle, PA. [NA, OF]

197. Friday, Moses. The morning and evening star. The Carlisle Arrow 7:15:4
      (December 16, 1910). Carlisle, PA. [NA, OF]

198. Friday, Moses. Ancient customs of Arapahoes. The Carlisle Arrow 7:39:4
      (June 2, 1911). Carlisle, PA. [MG, NA]

199. Fritschel, Erwin G. A history of the Indian mission of the Lutheran Iowa
      Synod, 1856 to 1866. M.A. thesis (Social Studies), Colorado State College
      of Education. Greeley, CO, 1939. xi + 182 pp. [EH, R]

200. Fritz, Henry E. The making of Grant's "Peace Policy." The Chronicles of
      Oklahoma 37:411-432 (1959). [EH, SA, TL]

201. Gabriel, Ralph Henry. The lure of the frontier; a story of race conflict.
      The pageant of America, Vol. 2. New Haven, CT: Yale University Press, 1929.
      327 pp. [EH]

202. Gallatin, Albert. A synopsis of the Indian tribes within the United States
      east of the Rocky Mountains, and in the British and Russian Possessions in
      North America. Transactions and Collections of the American Antiquarian
      Society 2:1-422. Cambridge, MA, 1836. [L, MG]

203. Gallatin, Albert. Hale's Indians of North-west America, and vocabularies of
      North America, with an Introduction. Transactions of the American Ethno-
      logical Society 2:xxiii-130. New York, NY: Bartlett and Welford, 1848. [L]

204. Garcia, Tanislado. A study on the effects of education upon the Arapaho
      Indians of the Wind River Reservation. M.A. thesis (Physical Education),
      University of Wyoming. Laramie, WY, 1965. vi + 91 pp. [CC, ME, MG, NA]

205. Garfield, Marvin H. Defense of the Kansas frontier, 1864-'65. The Kansas
      Historical Quarterly 1:140-152 (1931-1932). [EH]

206. Garfield, Marvin H. Defense of the Kansas frontier, 1866-1867. The Kansas
      Historical Quarterly 1:326:344 (1931-1932). [EH]

207. Garfield, Marvin H. Defense of the Kansas frontier, 1868-1869. The Kansas
      Historical Quarterly 1:451-473 (1931-1932). [EH]

208. Garrard, Lewis H. Wah-to-yah and the Taos Trail. Ed. by Ralph P. Bieber.
      (The Southwest Historical Series VI.) Glendale, CA: The Arthur H. Clark
      Company, 1938. 377 pp. + map. [EH]

209. Gatchet, Albert S. "Real," "true," or "genuine," in Indian languages. Ameri-
      can Anthropologist 1(n.s.):155-161 (1899). [L]

210. The General Miles collection of Indian relics. Art and Archaeology 21:273-278
      (1926). [DA, MC, PD]

211. Ghent, W. F. Friday. In Dictionary of American biography. Allen Johnson and
      Dumas Malone, eds. Vol. IV, Part 1: Fraunces - Grimke, p. 31. New York, NY:
      Charles Scribner's Sons (1931-32, 1959-60). [LH, NA]

212. Ghost dance song—Arapaho. The Southern Workman 36:111 (1907). Hampton, VA:
      Hampton Institute. [M]

213. Gill, Sam D. Native American traditions; sources and interpretations. Belmont, CA: Wadsworth Publishing Company, 1983. xiii + 183 pp. [R]

214. Githens, John H., Henry K. Knock, and William E. Hathaway. Prevalence of abnormal hemoglobins in American Indian children; survey in the Rocky Mountain area. The Journal of Laboratory and Clinical Medicine 57:755-758 (1961). [MB, NA]

215. Gittinger, Roy. The formation of the state of Oklahoma (1803-1906). University of California Publications in History, Vol. 6. Berkeley, CA: University of California Press, 1917. xii + 256 pp. [EH, SA, TL]

216. Gittinger, Roy. The formation of the state of Oklahoma, 1803-1906. Norman, OK: University of Oklahoma Press, 1939. xii + 309 pp. [EH, SA, TL]

217. Goddard, Ives. Sketch of Arapaho linguistic history. Unpublished MS, 1965. 48 pp. [L]

218. Goddard, Ives. Notes on the genetic classification of the Algonquian languages. National Museum of Canada, Bulletin 214, Anthropological Series No. 78, Contributions to Anthropology: Linguistics I (Algonquian), pp. 7-12. Ottawa: National Museum of Canada, 1967. [L]

219. Goddard, Ives. An outline of the historical phonology of Arapaho and Atsina. International Journal of American Linguistics 40:102-116 (1974). [L]

220. Goddard, Ives. The morphologization of Algonquian consonant mutation. Proceedings of the Third Annual Meeting of the Berkeley Linguistics Society, pp. 241-250. Berkeley, CA, 1977. [L]

221. Goddard, Ives. The evidence for Eastern Algonquian as a genetic subgroup. Algonquian Linguistics 5:2:19-22 (November 1979). [L]

222. Goddard, Ives. Comparative Algonquian. In The languages of native America; historical and comparative assessment. Lyle Campbell and Marianne Mithun, eds. Pp. 70-132. Austin, TX, 1979. [L]

223. Goddard, Ives. Against the linguistic evidence claimed for some Algonquian dialectal relationships. Anthropological Linguistics 23:7:271-297 (October 1981). [L]

224. Goff, Sue, and Tom DeVito. A background and history of St. Michael's Mission with the Arapaho people. [iii +] 140 pp. [+ 8 pp. of maps and 10 pp. of ills.] [Manuscript, 1979.] [CC, EH, IR, ME, MG, NA, OF, PD, R, V]

225. Goggles, Robert J., and others, trans. He nun na aie - Nee he dun na (The Arapahoe Dictionary). [94 pp.] [n.d.] [L, NA]

226. Grinnell, George Bird. Review of Goerge A. Dorsey and Alfred L. Kroeber, Traditions of the Arapaho. American Anthropologist 6:548-550 (1904).

227. Grinnell, George Bird. The fighting Cheyennes. New York, NY: Charles Scribner's Sons, 1915. viii + 431 pp. [EH, IR, NA, TL]

228. Grinnell, George Bird. Bent's Old Fort and its builders. Collections of the Kansas State Historical Society 15:28-91 (1919-1922). [EH]

229. Grinnell, George Bird. The Cheyenne Indians, their history and ways of life. New Haven, CT: Yale University Press, 1923. New York, NY: Cooper Square Publishers, 1962. Vol. 1 (xix + 359 pp.) and Vol. 2 (vii + 430 pp.). [EH, IR, NA, PD, TL]

230. Gross, Feliks. Nomadism of the Arapaho Indians of Wyoming and conflict between economics and idea system. Ethnos 14:65-88 (1949). [BE, CA, CC, MC, NA, PD, V]

231. Gross, Feliks. Nomadism of the Arapaho Indians of Wyoming, change in tech-
      nology, and its effects on the value system. University of Wyoming Publi-
      cations 15:3:37-55. Laramie, WY, 1950. [BE, CA, CC, MC, NA, PD, V]

232. Gross, Feliks. Language and value changes among the Arapaho. International
      Journal of American Linguistics 17:10-17 (1951). [CC, L, NA, V]

233. Guenther, Amalia Helen. The Cheyenne and Arapaho Indian reservation in Okla-
      homa. M.A. thesis (History), University of Oklahoma. Norman, OK, 1929.
      i + 118 pp. [EH, RE, SA, TL]

234. Gussow, Zachary. An ethnological report on Cheyenne and Arapaho: aboriginal
      occupation. In Arapaho-Cheyenne Indians. Pp. 27-95. New York, NY: Garland
      Publishing, 1974. [EH, MG]

235. Hafen, Ann Woodbury. Efforts to recover the stolen son of chief Ouray. The
      Colorado Magazine 16:53-62 (1939). [EH, PD]

236. Hafen, LeRoy R. Colorado; the story of a Western commonwealth. New York, NY:
      AMS Press, 1933, 1970. 328 pp. [EH, PD]

237. Hafen, LeRoy R. Fort St. Vrain. The Colorado Magazine 29:249-255 (1952).
      [EH, PD]

238. Hafen, LeRoy R. Friday, the Arapaho. In The mountain men and the fur trade
      of the Far West. LeRoy R. Hafen, ed. Vol. 8, pp. 185-192. Glendale, CA:
      The Arthur H. Clark Company, 1971. [EH, LH, NA]

239. Hafen, LeRoy R. Historical background and development of the Arapaho-Cheyenne
      land area. [i +] 69 [+ iii pp.] [Mimeographed, n.d.] [EH, IR, TL]

240. Hafen, LeRoy R. Historical background and development of the Arapaho-Cheyenne
      land area. In Arapaho-Cheyenne Indians. Pp. 97-173. New York, NY: Garland
      Publishing, 1974. [EH, IR, TL]

241. Hafen, LeRoy R., and W. J. Ghent. Broken Hand; the life story of Thomas Fitz-
      patrick, chief of the mountain men. Denver, CO: The Old West Publishing
      Company, 1931. [LH, NA]

242. Hafen, LeRoy R., and Ann W., eds. Relations with the Indians of the Plains,
      1857-1861; a documentary account of the military campaigns, and negotiations
      of Indian agents—with reports and journals of P. G. Lowe, R. M. Peck, J. E.
      B. Stuart [,] S. D. Sturgis, and other official papers. (The Far West and
      the Rockies, Vol. 9.) Glendale, CA: The Arthur H. Clark Company, 1959.
      310 pp. [EH, PD, TL]

243. Hafen, LeRoy R., and Ann W. Hafen, eds. Powder River campaigns and Sawyers
      expedition of 1865; a documentary account comprising official reports,
      diaries, contemporary newspaper accounts, and personal narratives. (The
      Far West and the Rockies historical series, 1820-1875, Vol. XII.) Glendale,
      CA: The Arthur H. Clark Company, 1961. 386 pp. + map. [EH]

244. Hafen, LeRoy R., and Francis Marion Young. Fort Laramie and the pageant of the
      West, 1834-1890. Glendale, CA: The Arthur H. Clark Company, 1938. 429 pp.
      [EH, MG, TL]

245. Hagerty, Leroy W. Indian raids along the Platte and Little Blue rivers, 1864-
      1865. M.A. thesis (History), University of Nebraska. Lincoln, NE, 1927.
      vii + 141 pp. [EH]

246. Haines, Elijah M. The American Indian (Uh-nish-in-na-ba). Chicago, IL: The
      Mas-sin-na'-gan Company, 1888. [L, OF]

247. Haines, Francis. The Plains Indians. New York, NY: Thomas Y. Crowell Company,
      1976. 213 pp. [EH, IR]

248. Hampton, James E. Pernicious anemia in American Indians. Journal of the
     Oklahoma State Medical Association 53:503-509 (1960). [MB, SA]

249. [Hand, James]. Northern Arapaho. [64 pp.] [1962] [EH, MG, NA, PS, R]

250. Harmon, E. M. The story of the Indian fort near Granby, Colorado. The Colo-
     rado Magazine 22:167-171 (1945). [EH]

251. Harper, R. H. Life and work among the Cheyennes and Arapahoes. New York, NY:
     American Missionary Association, [n.d.]. [7 pp.] [MG, R]

252. Harsha, William Justin. Neatha and the White-Man's-Bird. The Southern Workman
     30:578-586 (1901). Hampton, VA: Hampton Institute. [F]

253. Hart, Sheila, and Vada F. Carlson. We saw the sun dance; a story of the
     ancient religious ceremonial rite of the Shoshone and Arapaho Indians of
     Wyoming. 1948. 19 pp. [NA, R]

254. Hartmann, Horst. Die Plains- und Prärieindianer Nordamerikas. Veröffent-
     lichungen des Museums für Völkerkunde, Neue Folge 22. Berlin, 1973. 422 pp.
     [MG, PD]

255. Hasse, James Walter. Northern Arapahoe religious reorganization. M.A. thesis
     (Research), Saint Louis University. St. Louis, MO, 1965. vi + 150 pp.
     [BE, CA, CC, MG, NA, R, V]

256. Hayden, F. V. On the ethnography and philology of the Indian tribes of the
     Missouri Valley. Transactions of the American Philosophical Society, held
     at Philadelphia, for promoting useful knowledge. Vol. 12 (n.s.), pp. 231-
     461. Philadelphia, PA, 1863. [EH, L]

257. Haynes, Terry L. Recent trends in family planning on the Wind River Reserva-
     tion in Wyoming. [10 pp.] Manuscript, 1976. [CA, H, NA]

258. haynes, Terry L. Contraceptive behavior among Wind River Shoshone and Arapahoe
     females. M.A. thesis (Anthropology), Colorado State University. Fort Col-
     lins, CO, 1976. xi + 153 pp. [CC, H, MB, MG, NA]

259. Haynes, Terry L. Some factors related to contraceptive behavior among Wind
     River Shoshone and Arapahoe females. Human Organization 36:72-76 (1977).
     [CA, MB, NA]

260. Hebard, Grace Raymond. Washakie; an account of Indian resistance of the
     covered wagon and Union Pacific railroad invasions of their territory.
     Cleveland, OH: The Arthur H. Clark Company, 1930. 337 pp. [EH, IR, NA]

261. Hebard, Grace Raymond, and E. A. Brininstool. The Bozeman Trail: historical
     acounts of the blazing of the overland routes into the Northwest, and the
     fights with Red Cloud's warriors. Glendale, CA: The Arthur H. Clark Company,
     [1922], 1960. 2 volumes in 1: 346 pp., 306 pp. [EH, NA]

262. Heilman, Barbara. Farewell to Shannon Brown. Sports Illustrated 14:13:70-72,
     75-77, 79, 81-82 (April 3, 1961). Chicago, IL. [G, ME, NA, PD]

263. Henderson, Arn, and Richard D. Bauman. Indian environmental studies: the
     Cheyenne and Arapaho tribes of Oklahoma. [n.d.]. 68 pp. [BE, CA, EH, MG,
     PD, SA]

264. Henderson, Junius, and others. Colorado: short studies of its past and present.
     Boulder, CO: University of Colorado, 1927. x + 202 pp. [Chapter 2, by E. B.
     Renaud.] [MC, MG]

265. Henry, Joseph. Catholic missionaries on the Wind River: the Saint Stephen's
     Mission to the Arapahoes, 1884-1911. M.A. thesis (History), University of
     Wisconsin. Milwaukee, WI, 1984. [iii +] 95 pp. [CC, EH, ME, MG, NA, R]

266. Hilger, Sister M. Inez. Arapaho child life and its cultural background.
     Smithsonian Institution, Bureau of American Ethnology, Bulletin 148. Wash-
     ington, DC: GPO, 1952. xv + 253 pp. [CT, D, EH, H, L, MG, PD, PS, R, S, V]

267. History and economy of the Indians of the Wind River Reservation, Wyoming.
     Department of the Interior, Bureau of Indian Affairs, Missouri River Basin
     Investigations, Report No. 106. Billings, MT, 1950. 16pp. + 12 pp.(app.)
     [Mimeographed.] [BE, EH, NA]

268. Hockett, Charles F. Sapir on Arapaho. International Journal of American
     Linguistics 12:243-245 (1946). [L]

269. Hoebel, E. Adamson. The Plains Indians; a critical bibliography. Bloomington,
     IN: Indiana University Press, 1977. x + 75 pp. [B]

270. Hoig, Stan. The Sand Creek massacre. Norman, OK: University of Oklahoma Press,
     1961. xiii + 217 pp. [EH, PD]

271. Holbrook, Jeffery. Appraisal of Cheyenne-Arapahoe Indian lands located in
     eastern Colorado, western Kansas, southwestern Nebraska, southeastern Wyo-
     ming; valuation date: October 14, 1865. Portland, OR, [1958?]. 105 pp.
     [of typescript]. [EH, PD, RE, TL]

272. Holmgren, Charles A. Problematic alcohol use and alienation: a cross-cultural
     comparison between Indian and Caucasian high school students. Ph.D. disser-
     tation (Psychology), University of Wyoming. Laramie, WY, 1980. vii + 71 pp.
     [H, NA, P, V]

273. Holmgren, Charles, B. J. Fitzgerald, and Roderick S. Carman. Alienation and
     alcohol use by American Indian and Caucasian high school students. The
     Journal of Social Psychology 120:139-140 (1983). [H, NA, P, V]

274. Hook, Sidney. Methodological considerations in primitive art. The Open Court
     40:328-339 (1926). [DA]

275. Hopper, Ralph. Stories from Yellow Calf. [Collected by Frances Goggles.]
     [Wyoming, n.d.] [vii +] 21 pp. [LH, NA, OF, PD]

276. Howbert, Irving. The Indians of the Pike's Peak region; including an account
     of the battle of Sand Creek, and of occurrences in El Paso County, Colorado,
     during the war with the Cheyennes and Arapahoes, in 1864 and 1868. New York:
     NY: The Knickerbocker Press, 1914. Reprinted by The Rio Grande Press, Inc.,
     Glorieta, NM, 1970. x + 238 pp. [EH, IR, MG]

277. Howbert, Irving. Memories of a lifetime in the Pike's Peak region. New York,
     NY: G. P. Putnam's Sons, 1925. Reprinted by The Rio Grande Press, Inc.,
     Glorieta, NM, 1970. vi + 325 pp. [EH, IR]

278. Hoyt, Homer. Appraisal of Cheyenne and Arapaho Indian lands covering parts of
     the states of Colorado, Kansas, Wyoming and Nebraska [as of] October 14, 1865.
     Washington, DC, 1958. 214 pp. + appendices [of typescript]. [EH, PD, RE,
     TL]

279. Hultkrantz, Åke. Some notes on the Arapaho sun dance. Ethnos 17:24-38.
     Stockholm: The Ethnographical Museum of Sweden, 1952. [PD, R]

280. Hultkrantz, Åke. Conceptions of the soul among North American Indians; a
     study in religious ethnology. The Ethnographical Museum of Sweden, Stock-
     holm, Monograph Series, Publication No. 1. Stockholm, 1953. [R]

281. Hultkrantz, Åke. Prairie and Plains Indians. Institute of Religious Iconog-
     raphy, State University of Groningen. Iconography of religions, Section X:
     North America, Fasc. 2. Leiden, The Netherlands: E. J. Brill, 1973. [PD,
     R]

282. Humfreville, J. Lee. Twenty years among our hostile Indians; describing the characteristics, customs, habits, religion, marriages, dances and battles of the wild Indians in their natural state, together with the entrance of civilization through their hunting grounds, also the fur companies, overland stage, pony express, electric telegraph, and other phases of life in the pathless regions of the wild West. New York, NY: Hunter and Company, 1899. xxxvi + 45-479 pp. [EH, MG, PD]

283. Hungry Wolf, Adolf. Good medicine; companion issue. Fort MacLeod, Alberta: Good Medicine Books, 1971. [28 pp.] [M, PD, R]

284. Hunter, Bonnie. These Americans in moccasins. New York, NY: Vantage Press, 1959. [iv +] 13-67 pp. [F]

285. Hunter, Sara. Northern Arapahoe grandparents: traditional concepts and contemporary socio-economics. M.A. thesis (Anthropology), Indiana University. Bloomington, IN, 1977. iv + 130 pp. [BE, CA, K, NA, PS]

286. Hurst, C. T. Colorado's old-timers: the Indians back to 25,000 years ago. Southwestern Lore 12:18-26 (1946). [MG]

287. Hyde, George E. Life of George Bent written from his letters. Norman, OK: University of Oklahoma Press, 1968. xxv + 389 pp. [EH, IR]

288. Indian curriculum materials. Anadarko, OK: Bureau of Indian Affairs, Anadarko Area Office. 1980 [rev.]. 322 pp. [IM, MG, PD, SA]

289. The Indian treaty of April 1896. Annals of Wyoming 8:539-545 (1931). [EH, NA, TL]

290. Indians of Montana and Wyoming. Washington, DC: GPO, [1966, 1968.] 20 pp. [CA, CC, MG, SA, PD]

291. Indians of Oklahoma. Washington, DC: GPO, [1965, 1968]. 14, 16 pp. [CA, CC, MG, SA, PD]

292. Indians of Wyoming. League of Women Voters of Wyoming Publication No. 35. 4 pp. [Mimeographed, 1974?]. [CC, EH, IR, MG, NA, TL]

293. Jackson, W. H. Descriptive catalogue of photographs of North American Indians. [U.S.] Department of the Interior, United States Geological Survey of the Territories, Miscellaneous Publications, No. 9. Washington, DC: GPO, 1877. vi + 124 pp. [PD]

294. Johnson, Alice M., ed. Saskatchewan journals and correspondence; Edmonton House 1795-1800; Chesterfield House 1800-1802. Publications of Hudson's Bay Record Society XXVI. London: The Hudson's Bay Record Society, 1967. [EH, IR, NA]

295. Jones, Douglas C. The Treaty of Medicine Lodge; the story of the great treaty council as told by eyewitnesses. Norman, OK: University of Oklahoma Press, 1966. xv + 237 pp. [EH, MG, NA, PD, TL]

296. Jones, Douglas C. Medicine Lodge revisited. The Kansas Historical Quarterly 35:130-142 (1969). [EH, SA]

297. Judson, Katherine Berry. Myths and legends of the Great Plains. Chicago, IL: A. C. McClurg & Company, 1913. [OF]

298. Kappler, Charles J., comp. Indian affairs. Laws and treaties. 5 vols. Washington, DC: GPO, 1904, 1913, 1922, 1941. [TL]

299. Kate, H. F. C. ten. Reizen en onderzoekingen in Noord-Amerika. Leiden: E. J. Brill, 1885. [MG, SA]

300. Kaufman, Edmund George. The development of the missionary and philanthropic interest among the Mennonites of North America. Ph.D. dissertation (Practical Theology), University of Chicago. Chicago, IL, 1928. xiv + 504 pp. [EH, R]

301. Kaufman, Edmund G. Mennonite missions among the Oklahoma Indians. The Chronicles of Oklahoma 40:41-54 (1962). [EH, PD, R, SA]

302. Kaysbier, Fred. The new Indian generation. ...in Wyoming 6:6:8-10 (May-June 1974). Douglas, WY. [ME, NA, PD, R]

303. Kehoe, Alice B. The function of ceremonial sexual intercourse among the northern Plains Indians. Plains Anthropologist, Vol. 15, No. 48, pp. 99-103 (1970). [R, SA]

304. [Kingman, Samuel A.]. Diary of Samuel A. Kingman at Indian treaty in 1865. The Kansas Historical Quarterly 1:442-450 (1931-1932). [EH, TL]

305. Kneale, Albert H. Indian agent. Caldwell, ID: The Caxton Printers, 1950. 429 pp. [CC, EH, ME, NA, PD, SA]

306. Koch, Ronald Peter. Dress clothing of the Plains Indians. Norman, OK: University of Oklahoma Press, 1977. xvii + 219 pp. [DA, MC, MG, PD]

307. Kramský, Jiří. A quantitative typology of languages. Language and Speech 2:2:72-85 (1959). [L]

308. Kroeber, Alfred L. Symbolism of the Arapaho Indians. Bulletin of the American Museum of Natural History 13:69-86 (1900). New York, NY. [DA, MC, PD, SA]

309. Kroeber, A. L. The symbolism of the Arapaho Indians. Scientific American Supplement, No. 1297, Vol. 50, pp. 20784-20785 (November 10, 1900). New York, NY. [DA, R, SA]

310. Kroeber, Alfred Louis. Decorative symbolism of the Arapaho. Ph.D. dissertation (Anthropology), Columbia University. New York, NY, 1901. [DA, MC, PD]

311. Kroeber, A. L. Decorative symbolism of the Arapaho. American Anthropologist 3(n.s.):308-336 (1901). [DA, MC, PD]

312. Kroeber, Alfred L. The Arapaho: I. General description; II. Decorative art and symbolism. Bulletin of the American Museum of Natural History 18:1:1-150 (1902). New York, NY. [DA, K, L, MC, MG, PD, PS, R, S]

313. Kroeber, Alfred L. The Arapaho: III. Ceremonial organization. Bulletin of the American Museum of Natural History 18:2:151-229 (1904). New York, NY. [DA, L, MC, PD, PS, R]

314. Kroeber, Alfred L. The Arapaho: IV. Religion. Bulletin of the American Museum of Natural History 18:4:279-454 (1907). New York, NY. [DA, L, MC, PD, R]

315. Kroeber, A. L. Arapaho dialects. University of California Publications in American Archaeology and Ethnology 12:3:71-138. Berkeley, CA: University of California Press, 1916. [L, OF]

316. Kroeber, A. L. Cultural and natural areas of native North America. University of California Publications in American Archaeology and Ethnology, Vol. 38. Berkeley, CA: University of California Press, 1939. xii + 242 pp., maps. [MG]

317. Kroeber, Alfred L. The Arapaho. Lincoln, NE: University of Nebraska Press, 1983. xx + 1-229, 279-463 + plates. [Reprint of Nos. 312-314.] [DA, K, L, MC, MG, PD, PS, R, S]

318. Kroeker, Marvin. Colonel W. B. Hazen in the Indian Territory, 1868-1869. The Chronicles of Oklahoma 42:53-73 (1964). [EH, MG, SA, TL]

319. Kruse, Babs. Arapaho language. Thinking about sounds; an introduction to language learning. Student workbook. Ethete, WY: Wyoming Indian High School, 1982. [13 pp.] [IM, L, PD]

320. Kruse, Babs. Arapaho language [No. 3]. Arapaho alphabet. Student workbook.
     Ethete, WY: Wyoming Indian High School, 1982. [31 pp.] [IM, L, NA, PD]

321. Kruse, Babs, comp. The Wind River Reservation, 1865-1910; historical photo-
     graphs and anecdotes. Ethete, WY: Wyoming Indian High School, 1984.
     [28 pp.] [EH, IM, IR, LH, MG, NA, PD, TL]

322. Kruse, Babs, and Martha Woodenlegs. Arapaho language [No. 4]. Arapaho ani-
     mals. Student workbook. Ethete, WY: Wyoming Indian High School, 1982.
     [18 pp. + 15 pp. of teacher's supplement]. [IM, L, NA, PD]

323. Kruse, Babs, and Martha Woodenlegs. Arapaho language [No. 5]. Arapaho foods.
     Student workbook. Ethete, WY: Wyoming Indian High School, 1983. 33 pp.
     [+ 17 pp. of teacher's supplement]. [FP, IM, L, MC, PD]

324. Kruse, Babs, Martha Woodenlegs, and Wayne C'Hair. Arapaho language [No. 4].
     Arapaho animals. Student workbook. Ethete, WY: Wyoming Indian High School,
     1982. [34 pp.] [IM, L, NA, PD]

325. LaBarre, Weston. The peyote cult [enlarged ed.]. The Shoe String Press, 1970.
     [IR, R]

326. Lah, Ronald Leopold. Ethnoaesthetics of Northern Arapaho Indian music. Ph.D.
     dissertation (Anthropology), Northwestern University. Evanston, IL, 1980.
     ix + 304 pp. [M, MG, NA, V]

327. Lambert, Julia S. Plain tales of the Plains; Chapter V: Fortifying the com-
     missary and quartermaster's buildings--Lee's surrender--the volunteers
     mustered out--the treaty on the Little Arkansas. The Trail 9:1:16-24
     (June 1916). Denver, CO. [LH, MG, PD, TL]

328. Larson, T. A. History of Wyoming. 2nd ed., revised. Lincoln, NE: Univer-
     sity of Nebraska Press, [1965,] 1978. xi + 663 pp. [EH, IR, NA]

329. Latham, Robert Gordon. On the languages of New California. Proceedings of
     the Philological Society [of London] for 1852 and 1853, Vol. 6, No. 134,
     pp. 72-86 (May 13, 1853). London, 1854. [L]

330. Latham, R. G. On the languages of northern, western, and central America.
     Transactions of the Philological Society [of London for] 1856. Pp. 57-115.
     London: George Bell, [1857]. [L]

331. Latham, Robert Gordon. Opuscula. Essays chiefly philological and ethno-
     graphical. "On the languages of northern, western, and central America."
     Pp. 326-377. London: Williams and Norgate, 1860. [L]

332. Lathan, R. G. Elements of comparative philology. London: Walton and Maberly,
     1862. [L]

333. Law, Howard W. Rank fused person morphemes and matrix methodology in Arapaho
     (Algonkin). Linguistics: An International Review, No. 75, pp. 5-30. The
     Hague, 1971. [L]

334. Leacock, Eleanor. Some aspects of the philosophy of the Cheyenne and Arapaho
     Indians. M. A. thesis (Anthropology), Columbia University. New York, NY,
     1946. 46 pp. [OF, R, V]

335. Leacock, Eleanor, and June Nash. Ideologies of sex: archetypes and stereo-
     types. In Issues in cross-cultural research. Leonore Loeb Adler, ed.
     Annals of the New York Academy of Sciences. Vol. 285, pp. 618-645. New
     York, NY, 1977. [MG, OF, P, PS, V]

336. Leacock, Eleanor, and June Nash. Ideologies of sex: archetypes and stereo-
     types. In Cross-cultural research at issue. Leonore Loeb Adler, ed.
     Pp. 193-207. New York, NY: Academic Press, 1982. [MG, OF, P, PS, V]

337. Learning to speak their own language. The Wind River Rendezvous 9:6:9 (Novem-
      ber-December 1979). Saint Stephens, WY: Saint Stephens Indian Mission.
      (L, NA)

338. Leckie, William H. The military conquest of the Southern Plains Indians.
      Ph.D. dissertation (History), University of Oklahoma. Norman, OK, 1954.
      ix + 410 pp. [EH, SA]

339. Leitch, Barbara A. A concise dictionary of Indian tribes of North America.
      Reference Publications, 1979. Pp. 46-49. [MG, PD]

340. Lejeal, L. Review of Alfred L. Kroeber, The Arapaho. Journal de la Société
      des Américanistes de Paris 1(n.s.):348-350 (1904).

341. [Lemly, H. R.] Among the Arrapahoes. Harper's New Monthly Magazine, Vol. 60,
      No. 358, pp. 494-501 (March 1880). [EH, MG, NA, PD]

342. Lesser, Alexander. The Pawnee ghost dance hand game. New York, NY: Columbia
      University Press, 1933. x + 337 pp. [G, EH, IR, R]

343. Lévi-Strauss, Claude. Structuralism and ecology. Barnard Alumnae 61:3:6-14
      (Spring 1972). New York, NY. [OF, PD] [Reprinted in Readings in anthro-
      pology 77/78: Annual editions.]

344. Lévi-Strauss, Claude. The origin of table manners. (Introduction to a science
      of mythology, Vol. 3.) John and Doreen Weightman, trans. London: Jonathan
      Cape, 1978. 551 pp. [OF]

345. Lieurance, Thurlow. The musical soul of the American Indian. The etude
      38:10:655-656 (October 1920). [M]

346. Linderman, Frank B. American: the life story of a great Indian, Plenty-Coups,
      chief of the Crows. New York, NY: John Day Company, 1930. xi + 313 pp.
      [EH, IR, PD]

347. Linderman, Frank B. Plenty-coups; chief of the Crows. Lincoln, NE: Univer-
      sity of Nebraska Press, 1962. ix + 324 pp. [EH, IR, PD]

348. Linville, R. N. The Cheyenne and Arapahoe Indians of Oklahoma. M.A. thesis,
      Drake University. Des Moines, IA, [1905]. [72 pp.] [CC, EH, PS, R, SA]

349. Lopez, Barry Holstun. Winter count. New York, NY: Charles Scribner's Sons,
      1981. 112 pp. ["Buffalo," pp. 27-35.] [EH, NA, OF]

350. Lowie, Robert H. The test-theme in North American mythology. The Journal of
      American Folk-Lore 21:97-148 (1908). [OF, R]

351. Lowie, Robert H. Plains Indian age-societies: historical and comparative sum-
      mary. Anthropological Papers of the American Museum of Natural History
      11:13:877-1031. New York, NY, 1916. [IR, L, MG, PS, R]

352. Lowie, Robert H. Indians of the Plains. Anthropological Handbook No. 1,
      The American Museum of Natural History. New York, NY: McGraw-Hill Book
      Company, 1954. xv + 223 pp. Also published in the series American Museum
      Science Books. 1963. xx + 258 pp. [CC, EH, MG, PD]

353. Lubers, H. L. William Bent's family and the Indians of the Plains. The Colo-
      rado Magazine 13:19-22 (1936). [EH]

354. McCoy, Ron. Thieves' Road. Garden City, NY: Doubleday and Company, 1980.
      x + 176 pp. [EH, F, NA]

355. McCoy, Tim, with Ronald McCoy. Tim McCoy remembers the West; an autobiography.
      Garden City, NY: Doubleday and Company, 1977. x + 274 pp. [EH, LH, MG, NA,
      PD]

356. McLaughlin, James. My friend the Indian. Boston, MA: Houghton Mifflin Company, 1910. [EH, IR, NA, TL]

357. Mallery, Garrick. Sign language among North American Indians. First Annual Report of the Bureau of Ethnology to the Secretary of the Smithsonian Institution, 1879-'80. Pp. 263-552. Washington, DC: GPO, 1881. [L, P, PD]

358. Marriott, Alice, and Carol K. Rachlin. American Indian mythology. New York, NY: Crowell, 1968. xii + 211 pp. New York, NY: New American Library, 1972. 252 pp. [Pp. 187-193, 230-231.] [EH, OF]

359. Martin, John H., comp. List of documents concerning the negotiation of ratified Indian treaties [,] 1801-1869. Washington, DC: The National Archives, 1949. Special List No. 6. iii + 175 pp. [TL]

360. Meeker, Louis L. White Man. The Journal of American Folk-Lore 15:84-87 (1902). [OF]

361. Memories of "The People." The Wind River Rendezvous 11:1:10-11 (January-February 1981). Saint Stephens, WY: Saint Stephens Indian Mission. [EH, NA, PD]

362. Meriwether, Lee. A buckboard trip among the Indians. The Cosmopolitan 4:138-142 (October 1887). [MG]

363. Meserve, Charles Francis. The first allotment of lands in severalty among the Oklahoma Cheyenne and Arapahoe Indians. The Chronicles of Oklahoma 11:1040-1043 (1933). [BE, EH, SA]

364. Meyers, Ralph E. Delinquency among Wind River Reservation youth. M.A. thesis (Sociology), University of Wyoming. Laramie, WY, 1972. ix + 133 pp. [CA, IR, MG, NA, P, V]

365. Michelson, Truman. Preliminary report on the linguistic classification of Algonquian tribes. Twenty-eighth Annual Report of the Bureau of American Ethnology to the Secretary of the Smithsonian Institution [for] 1906-1907. Pp. 221-290b. Washington, DC: GPO, 1912. [L]

366. Michelson, Truman. The fundamental principles of Algonquian languages. Journal of the Washington Academy of Sciences 16:369-371 (1926). [L]

367. Michelson, Truman. Language studies among the Fox and Northern Arapaho Indians. Smithsonian Institution, Explorations and Field-work of the Smithsonian Institution in 1927 (Publication 2957), pp. 179-182. Washington, DC: GPO, 1928. [L, NA, PD]

368. Michelson, Truman. Algonquian Indian tribes of Oklahoma and Iowa. Smithsonian Institution, Explorations and Field-work of the Smithsonian Institution in 1928 (Publication 3011), pp. 183-188. Washington, DC: GPO, 1929. [L, SA]

369. Michelson, Truman. Linguistic miscellany. In Studies in honor of Hermann Collitz. Pp. 37-42. Baltimore, MD: The Johns Hopkins Press, 1930. [L]

370. Michelson, Truman. Studies of the Algonquian tribes of Iowa and Oklahoma. Smithsonian Institution, Explorations and Field-work of the Smithsonian Institution in 1929 (Publication 3060), pp. 207-212. Washington, DC: GPO, 1930. [L, SA]

371. Michelson, Truman. Narrative of an Arapaho woman. American Anthropologist 35:595-610 (1933). [LH, MG, SA]

372. Michelson, Truman. Anthropological studies in Oklahoma and Iowa. Smithsonian Institution, Explorations and Field-work of the Smithsonian Institution in 1932 (Publication 3213), pp. 89-92. Washington, DC: GPO, 1933. [L, PD]

373. Michelson, Truman. Some Arapaho kinship terms and social usages. American
      Anthropologist 36:137-139 (1934). [K, L]

374. Michelson, Truman. Phonetic shifts in Algonquian languages. International
      Journal of American Linguistics 8:131-171 (1935). [L]

375. Michener, James A. Centennial. New York, NY: Random House, 1974. 909 pp.
      Greenwich, CT: Fawcett Publications, 1975. 1087 pp. [F]

376. Mike Brown story-teller. The Wind River Rendezvous 4:6:1-3 (November-December
      1974). Saint Stephens, WY: Saint Stephens Indian Mission. [LH, NA, OF]

377. Miller, David Humphreys. Ghost dance. New York, NY: E. P. Dutton, 1959.
      Lincoln, NE: University of Nebraska Press, 1985. xviii + 318 pp. [EH, NA,
      R]

378. Miller, Horace Alden. Melodic views of Indian life; harmonization and adapta-
      tion of American Indian melodies. Chicago, IL: Clayton F. Summy, 1910.
      19 pp. [M]

379. Mitchell, Michael Dan. Acculturation problems among the Plains tribes of the
      government agencies in western Indian Territory. The Chronicles of Okla-
      homa 44:281-289 (1966). [CC, EH, SA]

380. Mollie and Mike "Iron Eyes." The Wind River Rendezvous 2:5:1-2 (September-
      October 1972). Saint Stephens, WY: Saint Stephens Indian Mission. [LH, NA]

381. Mooney, James. The ghost-dance religion and the Sioux outbreak of 1890.
      Fourteenth Annual Report of the Bureau of Ethnology, 1892-93. Part 2,
      pp. 641-1110. Washington, DC: GPO, 1896. [EH, L, M, PD, R]

382. Mooney, James. Calendar history of the Kiowa Indians. Seventeenth Annual
      Report of the Bureau of American Ethnology to the Secretary of the Smith-
      sonian Institution, 1895-96. Part I, pp. 129-445. Washington, DC: GPO,
      1898. [EH, IR, MG, PD]

383. Mooney, James. The Indian Congress at Omaha. American Anthropologist
      1(n.s.):126-149 (1899). [EH, L]

384. Mooney, James. Review of Alfred L. Kroeber, The Arapaho. American Anthro-
      pologist 5:126-130 (1903).

385. [Mooney, James]. Arapaho. In Handbook of American Indians north of Mexico.
      Frederick Webb Hodge, ed. Smithsonian Institution, Bureau of American
      Ethnology, Bulletin 30, Part 1, pp. 72-74. Washington, DC: GPO, 1907.
      (L, MG, PD)

386. [Mooney, James]. Basawunena. In Handbook of American Indians north of Mexico.
      Frederick Webb Hodge, ed. Smithsonian Institution, Bureau of American Eth-
      nology, Bulletin 30, Part 1, p. 132. Washington, DC: GPO, 1907. [MG]

387. [Mooney, James]. Hanahawunena. In Handbook of American Indians north of
      Mexico. Frederick Webb Hodge, ed. Smithsonian Institution, Bureau of Ameri-
      can Ethnology, Bulletin 30, Part 1, p. 530. Washington, DC: GPO, 1907. [MG]

388. [Mooney, James]. Little Raven. In Handbook of American Indians north of
      Mexico. Frederick Webb Hodge, ed. Smithsonian Institution, Bureau of Ameri-
      can Ethnology, Bulletin 30, Part 1, pp. 770-771. Washington, DC: GPO, 1907.
      [LH, SA]

389. [Mooney, James]. Nakasinena. In Handbook of American Indians north of Mexico.
      Frederick Webb Hodge, ed. Smithsonian Institution, Bureau of American Eth-
      nology, Bulletin 30, Part 2, p. 13. Washington, DC: GPO, 1910. [MG]

390. [Mooney, James]. Nawat. In Handbook of American Indians north of Mexico.
      Frederick Webb Hodge, ed. Smithsonian Institution, Bureau of American Eth-
      nology, Bulletin 30, Part 2, p. 46. Washington, DC: GPO, 1910. [LH, SA]

391. [Mooney, James]. Nawunena. In Handbook of American Indians north of Mexico. Frederick Webb Hodge, ed. Smithsonian Institution, Bureau of American Ethnology, Bulletin 30, Part 2, p. 47. Washington, DC: GPO, 1910. [MG, SA]

392. Mooney, James. The ghost-dance religion and the Sioux outbreak of 1890. Abridged, with an Introduction by Anthony F. C. Wallace. Chicago, IL: The University of Chicago Press, 1965. xxiii + 359 pp. [EH, L, M, PD, R]

393. Mooney, James. Calendar history of the Kiowa Indians. Introduction by John C. Ewers. Washington, DC: Smithsonian Institution Press, 1979. xiii + 129-460 pp. [EH, IR, MG, PD]

394. [Moran, P. ?]. Report on Indians taxed and Indians not taxed in the United States (except Alaska) at the Eleventh Census: 1890. [U.S.] Department of Interior, Census Office. Pp. 627-634. Washington, DC: GPO, 1894. [BE, MG, NA, PD]

395. Morgan, Lewis H. Systems of consanguinity and affinity of the human family. Smithsonian Contributions to Knowledge, Vol. 17. Washington, DC: Smithsonian Institution, 1871. [K, L]

396. Morris, Robert C. Wyoming Indians. A brief history, compiled from the United States census of 1890. Collections of the Wyoming Historical Society, Vol. I, pp. 91-108. Cheyenne, WY, 1897. [EH, IR, MG, NA, RE]

397. Morrow, Mable. Indian rawhide: an American folk art. (The Civilization of the American Indian Series, Vol. 132.) Norman, OK: University of Oklahoma Press, 1975. [DA, MC]

398. Munn, Nancy D. Visual categories: an approach to the study of representational systems. American Anthropologist 68:936-950 (1966). [DA]

399. Muntsch, Albert. Notes on age-classes among the Northern Arapaho. Primitive Man 5:49-52 (1932). [L, PS]

400. Murdock, George Peter, and Timothy J. O'Leary, comps. Arapaho. In Ethnographic bibliography of North America (4th edition). Human Relations Area Files, Behavior Science Bibliographies. Vol. 5: Plains and Southwest, pp. 30-35. New Haven, CT: Human Relations Area Files Press, 1975. [B]

401. Murdock, Margaret Maier. The political attitudes of Native American children: the Arapahoe and Shoshoni of the Wind River Reservation in Wyoming. Ph.D. dissertation (Political Science), Tufts University. Medford, MA, 1978. 390 pp. [CA, NA, P, PS, V]

402. Murphy, James C. The place of the Northern Arapahoes in the relations between the United States and the Indians of the Plains, 1851-1879. M.A. thesis (History), University of British Columbia. Vancouver, British Columbia, 1966. ix + 164 pp. [EH, IR, MG, NA]

403. Murphy, James C. The place of the Northern Arapahoes in the relations between the United States and the Indians of the Plains, 1851-1879. Annals of Wyoming 41:33-61, 203-259 (1969). [EH, NA, TL]

404. Nadeau, Remi. Fort Laramie and the Sioux Indians. Englewood Cliffs, NJ: Prentice-Hall, 1967. xiii + 335 pp. [EH, TL]

405. A narrative in words and pictures of the Church's work at St. Michael's Mission, Ethete, Wyoming. 1936. [30 pp.] [ME, NA, PD, R]

406. [Nash, M. B.]. Legends of the northern Wyoming Indians. The Billings Gazette, March 13, 1916. [MG, NA]

407. Native lands of the Arapaho and Shoshone. Saint Stephens, WY: Saint Stephens Indian School, 1978. [4 pp.] [EH, IM, NA]

408.   Nettl, Bruno.   Musical culture of the Arapaho.   M.A. thesis (Anthropology),
       Indiana University.   Bloomington, IN, 1951.   vi + 116 pp.   [D, L, M, MC, MG,
       NA, R]

409.   Nettl, Bruno.   Observations on meaningless peyote song texts.   Journal of Ameri-
       can Folklore 66:161-164 (1953), (No. 260).   [M, NA]

410.   Nettl, Bruno.   Stylistic variety in North American Indian music.   Journal of
       the American   Musicological Society 6:160-168 (1953).   [M, NA, PD]

411.   Nettl, Bruno.   Notes on musical composition in primitive culture.   Anthropo-
       logical Quarterly 27:81-90 (1954).   [M, NA]

412.   Nettl, Bruno.   Text-music relationships in Arapaho songs.   Southwestern Journal
       of Anthropology 10:192-199 (1954).   [L, M, NA]

413.   Nettl, Bruno.   Musical culture of the Arapaho.   The Musical Quarterly 41:325-
       331 (1955).   [M, NA]

414.   Nettl, Bruno.   Relaciones entre la lengua y la música en el folklore.   Folklore
       Américas 16:1:1-11 (1956).   [L, M, PD]

415.   Nettl, Bruno.   Zur Kompositionstechnik der Arapaho.   Jahrbuch für musikalische
       Volks- und Völkerkunde 2:114-118 (1966).   Berlin.   [L, M, NA]

416.   Nettl, Bruno.   In honor of our principal teachers.   Ethnomusicology 28:173-185
       (1984).   Ann Arbor, MI.   [LH, M, NA]

417.   Neuman, Robert W.   Porcupine quill flatteners from central United States.
       American Antiquity 26:99-102 (1960).   [MC, PD]

418.   Nickerson, H. G.   Early history of Fremont County.   State of Wyoming Histori-
       cal Department Quarterly Bulletin   2:1:1-13 (1924).   [EH, NA]

419.   [1984 calendar].   Ethete, WY: Wyoming Indian High School.   [1983].   [12 pp.]
       [Small format.]   [NA, PD]

420.   [1984 calendar].   Ethete, WY: Wyoming Indian High School.   [1983].   [12 pp.]
       [Large format.]   [NA, PD]

421.   [1986 calendar].   Ethete, WY: Wyoming Indian Elementary Wolf Dancers Club.
       [1985].   14 pp.   [PD]

422.   Northern Arapahoe tribe.   Fort Washakie, WY, [n.d.].   [76 pp.]   [BE, CA, CC,
       NA, PS]

423.   Nun-na-a-in-ah Ve-vith-ha Hin-nen-nau Hin-nen-it-dah-need.   [n.d.]   12 pp.
       [L, R]

424.   Nye, Wilbur Sturtevant.   Carbine and lance; the story of old Fort Sill (2nd
       revised edition).   Norman, OK: University of Oklahoma Press, 1937, 1942.
       xix + 345 pp.   [EH, IR, PD, TL]

425.   Olden, Sarah Emilia.   Shoshone folk lore; as discovered from the Rev. John
       Roberts, a hidden hero, on the Wind River Indian Reservation in Wyoming.
       Milwaukee, WI: Morehouse Publishing Company, 1923.   [NA, OF]

426.   Oliver, Symmes C.   Ecology and cultural continuity as contributing factors
       in the social organization of the Plains Indians.   University of California
       Publications in American Archaeology and Ethnology 48:1:1-90.   Berkeley,
       CA: University of California Press, 1962.   [EH, MG, PS, S]

427.   Painter, C. C.   Cheyennes and Arapahoes revisited and a statement of their
       agreement and contract with attorneys.   Philadelphia, PA: The Indian Rights
       Association, 1893.   62 pp.   [CC, EH, SA, TL]

428. Pajeken, Friedrich J. Die Umgangssprache der Arapahoe-Indianer. Das Ausland;
     Wochenschrift für Länder- und Völkerkunde 62:89-90 (1889). Stuttgart and
     München. [L]

429. Pajeken. Friedrich J. Religion und religiöse Vorstellungen der Arrapahoë-
     Indianer. Das Ausland; Wochenschrift für Erd- und Völkerkunde 63:1011-1015
     (1890). Stuttgart. [R]

430. Pannell, W. G. Arapahoes hold sun dance. Indians at Work 3:11:41-42
     (January 15, 1936). Washington, DC: U.S. Office of Indian Affairs. [R, SA]

431. Parkman, Francis, Jr. The California and Oregon Trail: being sketches of
     prairie and Rocky Mountain life. New York, NY: George P. Putnam, 1849.
     448 pp. [EH, IR]

432. Parsons, Eugene. The Indian and his problems. The Trail 6:6:5-9 (November
     1913). [MG, PD]

433. Peery, Dan W. The Indians' friend, John H. Seger. His stories of the myths,
     legends and religions of the Cheyenne and Arapaho tribes. The Chronicles
     of Oklahoma 10:348-368, 570-591, and 11:709-732, 845-868, 967-994 (1932-33).
     [CC, EH, MG, R, SA]

434. Pennington, William D. Government policy and Indian farming on the Cheyenne
     and Arapaho reservation: 1869-1880. The Chronicles of Oklahoma 57:171-189
     (1979). [EH, PD, RE, S, SA]

435. Penoi, Charles. No more buffaloes; the Cheyenne and Arapaho tribes of Oklahoma,
     Yukon, OK: Pueblo Publishing Press, 1981, 1982. 55 pp., 116 pp. [CA, EH, IR,
     MG, P, SA, V]

436. Pentland, David H. Causes of rapid phonological change: the case of Atsina and
     its relatives. Calgary Working Papers in Linguistics, No. 5, pp. 99-137
     (Spring 1979). Calgary, Alberta: Department of Linguistics, The University
     of Calgary. [L]

437. Pentland, David H., and H. Christoph Wolfart. Bibliography of Algonquian lin-
     guistics. Winnipeg, Manitoba: The University of Manitoba Press, 1982. xix
     + 333 pp. [B, L]

438. Pentland, David H., and others. A bibliography of Algonquian linguistics.
     University of Manitoba Anthropology Papers, No. 11. [ii +] 85 pp. Winnipeg,
     Manitoba, 1974 [B, L]

439. [The People]. The Wind River Rendezvous 8:5:1-16 (September-October 1978).
     Saint Stephens, WY: Saint Stephens Indian Mission. [CA, CC, EH, LH, NA, PD,
     R]

440. Perkins, Georgia B., and Gertrude M. Church. Report of pediatric evaluations
     of a sample of Indian children--Wind River Indian Reservation, 1957. Ameri-
     can Journal of Public Health and the Nation's Health 50:181-194 (1960).
     [H, MB, NA]

441. Perrigo, Lynn I. Major Hal Sayr's diary of the Sand Creek campaign. The Colo-
     rado Magazine 15:41-48 (1938). [EH, NA, PD]

442. Perry, Joseph M. Economic genocide: a study of the Comanche, Kiowa, Chevenne
     and Arapaho: a reaction. The Negro Educational Review 24:104-105 (1973).
     [BE, CA, EH, SA]

443. Photograph preservation project. Title IV-A Curriculum Development Department,
     Wyoming Indian High School. Ethete, WY, 1983. 83 pp. [NA, PD]

444. Picard, Marc. The phonological history of Arapaho: a study in linguistic
     change. Ph.D. dissertation (Linguistics), McGill University. Montreal,
     Quebec, 1975 [1977]. xii + 333 pp. [L]

445. Picard, Marc. Les regles morphophonemiques en diachronie. In Montreal Work-
      ing Papers in Linguistics. Henrietta Cedergren, Yves Charles Morin, and
      Glyne L. Piggott, eds. Vol. 8, pp. 129-136. Montreal, Quebec, 1977. [L]

446. Picard, Marc. The syllable boundary in generative phonology. Canadian Journal
      of Linguistics 24:119-131 (1979). [L]

447. Picard, Marc. A constraint on role complementation. Indiana University
      Linguistics Club. Bloomington, IN, 1980. 24 pp. [Mimeographed.] [L]

448. Picard, Marc. La phonologie historique de l'arapaho: nouvelles solutions à
      trois vieux problèmes. Montreal Working Papers in Linguistics, Vol. 16:
      Linguistique Amérindienne II: Études Algonquiennes, pp. 193-209. Lynn
      Drapeau, ed. Montreal: McGill University, 1981. [L]

449. Picard, Marc. Le changement naturel et le *ł du proto-algonquin. Montreal
      Working Papers in Linguistics, Vol. 16: Linguistique Amérindienne II: Études
      Algonquiennes, pp. 211-228. Lynn Drapeau, ed. Montreal: McGill University,
      1981. [L]

450. Picard, Marc. The case against Cheyenne n from PA *k. International Journal
      of American Linguistics 50:111-117 (1984). [L]

451. Picard, Marc. On the naturalness of Algonquian ł. International Journal of
      American Linguistics 50:424-437 (1984). [L]

452. Picard, Marc. On relative chronology and natural sound change. The McGill
      Working Papers in Linguistics 2:2:115-121. Montreal, Quebec: Department of
      Linguistics, McGill University, 1985. [L]

453. Pilling, James Constantine, comp. Bibliography of the Algonquian languages.
      Smithsonian Institution, Bureau of Ethnology, Bulletin 13. Washington, DC:
      GPO, 1891, [1892]. [B]

454. Post, George. Blood group studies on the Arapahoe and Shoshoni Indian tribes
      of Wyoming. M.A. thesis (Zoology and Physiology), University of Wyoming.
      Laramie, WY, 1948. iv + 66 pp. [MB, NA]

455. Pott, Friedrich August. Die Sprachverschiedenheit in Europa an den Zahl-
      wörtern nachgewiesen sowie die quinäre und vigesimale Zählmethode. Halle,
      1868. [L]

456. Proposed ten year program--Wind River Indian Reservation, 1946-1955 incl.
      U.S. Department of the Interior, Office of Indian Affairs. Circular No.3514.
      Fort Washakie, WY, 1943. [viii + 80 + i pp.] [Mimeographed.] [BE, NA, RE]

457. Proulx, Paul. Algonquian objective verbs. International Journal of American
      Linguistics 50:403-423 (1984). [L]

458. Putting the show on the road: Arapahoe. Instructor 82:6:51-53 (February 1973).
      [CA, ME, NA, PD]

459. Radin, Paul. The Winnebago tribe (Jesse Clay's account of the Arapaho manner
      of giving the peyote ceremony which he introduced among the Winnebago in
      1912.) Thirty-seventh Annual Report of the Bureau of American Ethnology to
      the Secretary of the Smithsonian Institution [for] 1915-1916. Pp. 415-419.
      Washington, DC: GPO, 1923. [IR, R, SA]

460. Rambo, Edward A. Appraisal of certain lands of the Cheyenne and Arapaho
      tribes located in northern and western Oklahoma; effective date of the ap-
      praisal--3 March 1891. Oklahoma City, OK, 1962. v + 145 pp. [of type-
      script]. [EH, PD, RE, SA, TL]

461. Rawlings, Charles. General Connor's Tongue River battle. Annals of Wyoming
      36:73-76 (1964). [EH, NA]

462. Rawlings, Charles. The Sawyer expedition. Annals of Wyoming 36:69-73 (1964).
      [EH, NA]

463. Rees, John E. Indian picture writing. Eleventh Biennial Report of the Board
      of Trustees of the State Historical Society of Idaho. Pp. 17-19. Boise, ID,
      1928. [G]

464. Reese, Jim E., and Mary Fish. Economic genocide: a study of the Comanche,
      Kiowa, Cheyenne and Arapaho. The Negro Educational Review 24:86-103 (1973).
      [BE, CA, EH, SA]

465. Reilly, Robert T. Wind River changes its course: the St. Stephens experience.
      Phi Delta Kappan 62:3:200-202 (November 1980). [CA, ME, NA, PD]

466. Report of the April 26, 1977 hearing on Indian civil rights issues in north-
      western Oklahoma. Oklahoma City, OK: Oklahoma Human Rights Commission,
      [1977?]. i + 50 pp. [CA, EH, MG, SA, TL]

467. Report of the council held by the President of the United States [Hayes], and
      all the visiting chiefs of the Sioux and Arapahoe tribes of Indians, Septem-
      ber 26, 1877, in Washington, D.C. Omaha, NE, 1877. 22 pp. [EH, NA, TL]

468. The restored reservation. Saint Stephens, WY: Saint Stephens Indian School,
      1978. [4 pp.] [EH, IM, NA]

469. Richardson, Albert D. Beyond the Mississippi: from the great river to the
      great ocean. Life and adventure on the prairies, mountains, and Pacific
      coast....1857-1867. Hartford, CT: American Publishing Company, 1867. xvi +
      17-572 pp. [EH, MG]

470. Richert, Bernhard Ernest. Plains Indians medicine bundles. M.A. thesis
      (Anthropology), University of Texas. Austin, TX, 1969. 209 pp. [MC, MG, R]

471. Robertson, Karen, ed. What's cooking? Saint Stephens, WY: Saint Stephens
      Indian School, 1977. 8 pp. [FP, IM, NA, PD]

472. Robinson, Maudie. Grass Singing, Indian bride of Kit Carson. Fort Worth, TX:
      Western Heritage Press, 1977. 192 pp. [EH, F, LH, PD]

473. Rogers, Frank K. The rain-dance of the Arapahoes and Cheyennes. The Southern
      Workman 29:721-723 (1900). [D, R, SA]

474. Rogers, Mary Louise. Curriculum planning for Cheyenne and Arapaho Indians.
      M.Ed. thesis, University of Oklahoma. Norman, OK, 1943. v + 118 pp.
      [BE, EH, ME, MG, SA]

475. Ross, Adeline R. Indian life in Wyoming. The Sewanee Review 19:61-70 (1911).
      [EH, IR, MG, NA]

476. Royce, Charles C., comp. Indian land cessions in the United States. Eighteenth
      Annual Report of the Bureau of American Ethnology to the Secretary of the
      Smithsonian Institution [for] 1896-'97. Pp. 521-964. Washington, DC:
      GPO, 1899. [EH, IR, TL]

477. Ruíz, José Francisco. Report on the Indian tribes of Texas in 1828. John C.
      Ewers, ed. Western Americana Series, No. 5. New Haven, CT: Yale University
      Library, 1972. [EH, MG]

478. Ruxton, George Frederick. Wild life in the Rocky Mountains; a true tale of
      rough adventure in the days of the Mexican War. [Ed. by Horace Kephart.]
      New York, NY: The Macmillan Company, 1916. 303 pp. [EH]

479. Ruxton, George Frederick. Mountain men; George Frederick Ruxton's firsthand
      accounts of fur trappers and Indians in the Rockies. [Ed. by Glen Rounds.]
      New York, NY: Holiday House, 1966. 278 pp. [EH, F]

480. Safar, Dwight. An exploratory study of mental maturity, achievement and
     personality test results in relation to the academic progress of Indians
     and non-Indians in grades four through eight in six public school districts
     and one parochial school in Fremont County, Wyoming. Ph.D. dissertation
     (Education), University of Wyoming. Laramie, WY, 1964. viii + 86 pp.
     [IR, ME, NA, P]

481. Sage, Rufus B. Rufus B. Sage: his letters and papers [,] 1836-1847 [,] with
     an annotated reprint of his "Scenes in the Rocky Mountains and in Oregon,
     California, New Mexico, Texas, and the Grand Prairies." LeRoy R. and Ann W.
     Hafen, eds. Vol. 2. (The Far West and the Rockies, Vol. 5.) Glendale, CA:
     The Arthur H. Clark Company, 1956. 361 pp. [EH, IR]

482. Salomon, Julian Harris. The book of Indian crafts & Indian lore. New York,
     NY: Harper & Brothers Publishers, 1928. [D, DA, M, MC]

483. Salzmann, Zdenek. An Arapaho version of the Star Husband tale. Hoosier
     Folklore 9:50-58 (1950). [NA, OF]

484. Salzmann, Zdenek. Contrastive field experience with language and values of
     the Arapaho. International Journal of American Linguistics 17:98-101 (1951).
     [CC, L, NA, V]

485. Salzmann, Zdenek. The problem of lexical acculturation. International
     Journal of American Linguistics 20:137-139 (1954). [L]

486. Salzmann, Zdenek. Arapaho I: phonology. International Journal of American
     Linguistics 22:49-56 (1956). [L, NA]

487. Salzmann, Zdenek. Arapaho II: texts. International Journal of American
     Linguistics 22:151-158 (1956). [L, NA, OF]

488. Salzmann, Zdenek. Arapaho III: additional texts. International Journal of
     American Linguistics 22:266-272 (1956). [L, NA, OF]

489. Salzmann, Zdenek. Arapaho tales III. Midwest Folklore 7:27-37 (1957). [NA,
     OF]

490. Salzmann, Zdenek. Arapaho kinship terms and two related ethnolinguistic ob-
     servations. Anthropological Linguistics 1:9:6-10 (1959). [K, L, NA]

491. Salzmann, Zdenek. Two brief contributions toward Arapaho linguistic history.
     Anthropological Linguistics 2:7:39-48 (1960). [L, NA]

492. Salzmann, Zdenek. Concerning the assumed l-sound in Arapaho. Plains Anthro-
     pologist, Vol. 6, No. 14, pp. 270-271 (1961). [L]

493. Salzmann, Zdenek. Bibliography of works on the Arapaho division of Algonquian.
     International Journal of American Linguistics 27:183-187 (1961). [B, L]

494. Salzmann, Zdenek. Arapaho IV: interphonemic specification. International
     Journal of American Linguistics 27:151-155 (1961). [L, NA]

495. Salzmann, Zdenek. A sketch of Arapaho grammar. Ph.D. dissertation (Anthro-
     pology), Indiana University. Bloomington, IN, 1963. vii + 169 pp. [L, NA]

496. Salzmann, Zdenek. Arapaho V: noun. International Journal of American Lin-
     guistics 31:39-49 (1965). [L, NA]

497. Salzmann, Zdenek. Arapaho VI: noun. International Journal of American
     Linguistics 31:136-151 (1965). [L, NA]

498. Salzmann, Zdenek. Arapaho VII: verb. International Journal of American
     Linguistics 33:209-223 (1967). [L, NA]

499. Salzmann, Zdenek. Some aspects of Arapaho morphology. National Museum of Canada, Bulletin No. 214, Anthropological Series No. 78, Contributions to Anthropology: Linguistics I (Algonquian). Pp. 128-134. Ottawa, 1967. [L, NA]

500. Salzmann, Zdenek. On the inflection of transitive animate verbs in Arapaho. National Museum of Canada, Bulletin No. 214, Anthropological Series No. 78, Contributions to Anthropology: Linguistics I (Algonquian). Pp. 135-139. Ottawa, 1967. [L, NA]

501. Salzmann, Zdenek. Salvage phonology of Gros Ventre (Atsina). International Journal of American Linguistics 35:307-314 (1969). [L, NA]

502. Salzmann, Zdenek, ed. and comp. Arapaho stories--Hinóno'éí hoo3ítóono. Anchorage, AK, 1980. iv + 100 pp. [L, NA, OF]

503. Salzmann, Zdenek, ed. Two traditional Arapaho tales. Arapaho Language and Culture Instructional Materials Series, No. 1. Wind River Reservation, WY, 1981. [i +] 50 pp. [NA, OF]

504. Salzmann, Zdenek. Analytical bibliography of sources concerning the Arapaho Indians. Arapaho Language and Culture Instructional Materials Series, No. 2. Wind River Reservation, WY, 1981. ii + 40 pp. [B, IM]

505. Salzmann, Zdenek. Bibliography of sources concerning the Arapaho language. Algonquian and Iroquoian Linguistics 7:3:37-41 (1982). [B, L]

506. Salzmann, Zdenek. Guest column in the Wind River News: Arapaho language in danger. Vol. I, No. 6, p. 5 (May 12, 1983). [L, ME, NA]

507. Salzmann, Zdenek. Guest column in the Wind River News: Drastic methods needed to save Arapaho language. Vol. 1, No. 7, p. 5 (May 17, 1983). [L, ME, NA]

508. Salzmann, Zdenek. Guest column in the Wind River News: Arapaho children prime choices to restore native language. Vol. 1, No. 8, p. 5 (May 24, 1983). [L, ME, NA]

509. Salzmann, Zdenek. Guest column in the Wind River News: Saving Arapaho language ends on positive note. Vol. 1, No. 9, p. 5 (May 31, 1983). [L, ME, NA]

510. Salzmann, Zdenek. Analytical bibliography of sources concerning the Arapaho Indians. 2nd ed., revised and expanded. Arapaho Language and Culture Instructional Materials Series, No. 3. Wind River Reservation, WY, 1983. iii + 51 pp. [B, IM]

511. Salzmann, Zdenek. Dictionary of contemporary Arapaho usage. Arapaho Language and Culture Instructional Materials Series, No. 4. Wind River Reservation, WY, 1983. v + 231 pp. [B, L, MG, NA]

512. Salzmann, Zdenek and Joy. Arapaho tales I. Hoosier Folklore 9:80-96 (1950). [NA, OF]

513. Salzmann, Zdenek and Joy. Arapaho tales II. Midwest Folklore 2:21-42 (1952). [NA, OF]

514. Sanders, Gledca S. The educational development of the Cheyenne and Arapaho Indians upon the reservation. M.S. thesis, Oklahoma Agricultural and Mechanical College. Stillwater, OK, 1933. vi + 85 pp. [CC, EH, ME, SA]

515. Sanford, D. A. Indian topics or, experiences in Indian missions with selections from various sources. New York, NY: Broadway Publishing Company, 1911. 108 pp. [EH, G, H, L, M, MG, PD, S, SA]

516. Sapir, Edward. The Algonkin affinity of Yurok and Wiyot kinship terms. Journal de la Société des Américanistes de Paris (n.s.) 15:36-74 (1923). [L]

517. Schmidt, P. Wilhelm. Der Ursprung der Gottesidee; eine historisch-kritische und positive Studie. Die Religionen der Urvölker Amerikas. Vol. 2, Part 2: Die Religionen der Urvölker I. Münster i. W., 1929. [R]

518. Schmidt, W. The origin and growth of religion; facts and theories. Translated from the German by H. J. Rose. London: Methuen & Co., 1931. [R]

519. Schmidt, W. High gods in North America. (Upton Lectures in Religion, Manchester College, Oxford, 1932.) Oxford: Clarendon Press, 1933. [R]

520. Schmidt, P. Wilhelm. Der Ursprung der Gottesidee; eine historisch-kritische und positive Studie. Nachträge zu den Religionen der Urvölker Amerikas, Asiens u. Australiens. Vol. 5, Part 2: Die Religionen der Urvölker IV. Münster i. W., 1934. [R]

521. Schmidt, P. Wilhelm. Der Ursprung der Gottesidee; eine historisch-kritische und positive Studie. Endsynthese der Religionen der Urvölker Amerikas, Asiens, Australiens, Afrikas. Vol. 6, Part 2: Die Religionen der Urvölker V. Münster i. W., 1935. [R]

522. Schmidt, Wilhelm. Das Tauchmotiv in Erdschöpfungsmythen Nordamerikas, Asiens und Europas. Mélanges de linguistique et de philologie offerts a Jacq. van Ginneken a l'occasion du soixantième anniversaire de sa naissance (21 avril 1937). Pp. 111-122. [OF]

523. Schmidt, P. Wilhelm. Der Ursprung der Gottesidee; eine historisch-kritische und positive Studie. Die afrikanischen Hirtenvölker: Hamiten und Hamitoiden. Vol. 7, Part 3: Die Religionen der Hirtenvölker. Münster i. W., 1940. [R]

524. Schoolcraft, Henry R. Historical and statistical information, respecting the history, condition and prospects of the Indian tribes of the United States: collected and prepared under the direction of the Bureau of Indian Affairs, per Act of Congress of March 3d, 1847. [Titles of the several parts vary somewhat.] Philadelphia, PA: [J. B.] Lippincott [, Grambo] and Company. Parts I-VI: xviii + 13-568 (1851), xxiv + 17-608 (1852), xviii + 19-635 (1853), xxvi + 19-668 (1854), xxiv + 25-712 (1855), xxviii + 25-756 (1857). [EH, L, MG, PD]

525. Schulte, Steven C. Indians and politicians: the origins of a "Western" attitude toward Native Americans in Wyoming 1868-1906. Annals of Wyoming 56:2-11 (1984). [EH, NA, PD, TL]

526. Schutz, W. D., J. L. Baker, and Andrew Vanvig. Indian ranching on the Wind River Reservation, Wyoming. Missouri River Basin Investigations Project, Bureau of Indian Affairs, United States Department of the Interior [under research contract with] Agricultural Experiment Station, University of Wyoming, Bulletin 366. Laramie, WY, 1960. 36 pp. [BE, NA, RE]

527. Scott, Hugh Lenox. The early history and the names of the Arapaho. American Anthropologist 9:545-560 (1907). [EH, IR, L]

528. Sears, Roscoe H. Appraisal of Cheyenne and Arapahoe Indian Reservation in the Indian Territory--State of Oklahoma, 1869. Oklahoma City, OK, [1962?]. 53 pp. [of typescript]. [EH, PD, RE, SA, TL]

529. Sears, Roscoe H. Appraisal of Cheyenne and Arapahoe Indian Reservation in the Indian Territory--State of Oklahoma, 1891. Oklahoma City, OK, [196?]. 89 pp. [of typescript]. [EH, PD, RE, SA, TL]

530. Seger, John H. Early days among the Cheyenne and Arapaho Indians. Edited by W. S. Campbell. University of Oklahoma Bulletin, University Series No. 281, University Studies No. 19. Norman, OK, 1924. 91 pp. [CC, EH, SA]

531. Seger, John H. Early days among the Cheyenne and Arapahoe Indians. Edited by Stanley Vestal. (The Civilization of the American Indian Series.) Norman, OK: University of Oklahoma Press, 1979. xvi + 145 pp. [CC, EH, PD, SA]

532. Shakespeare, Thomas. An Arapaho legend. The Wind River Rendezvous 8:4:7
     (July-August 1978). Saint Stephens, WY; Saint Stephens Indian Mission.
     [NA, OF]

533. Shakespeare, Tom. The Sky People. New York, NY: Vantage Press, 1971. 117 pp.
     [A, EH, LH, MG, NA, PS, R]

534. Shane, Ralph M. Centennial historical map [of the] Wind River Indian Reser-
     vation [,[1868-1968 [,] home of the Shoshones and Arapahoes. 1968. [EH,
     IR, MG, NA, PD, TL]

535. Shields, Lillian B. Relations with the Cheyennes and Arapahoes in Colorado to
     1861. The Colorado Magazine 4:145-154 (1927). [EH, IR, PD]

536. Shimkin, D. B. Wind River Shoshone ethnogeography. Anthropological Records,
     Vol. 5, No. 4, pp. v + 245-288. Berkeley, CA: University of California
     Press, 1947. [RE]

537. Shonle, Ruth. Peyote, the giver of visions. American Anthropologist 27:53-
     75 (1925). [EH, IR, PD, R]

538. Short, Anthony J. Indian power saves a school. Momentum: Journal of the
     National Catholic Educational Association 7:4:37-42 (December 1976). [CA,
     ME, NA]

539. [Short, Anthony, S. J.]. [Mission Centennial issue of] The Wind River Rendezvous
     14:2:1-24 (April-June 1984). Saint Stephens, WY: St. Stephen's Indian Mis-
     sion Foundation. [CC, EH, IR, LH, ME, MG, NA, PD, R]

540. [Short, Anthony, S. J.]. [Mission Centennial issue of] The Wind River Rendezvous
     14:3:1-24 (July-September 1984). Saint Stephens, WY: St. Stephen's Indian
     Mission Foundation. [CC, EH, IR, LH, ME, MG, NA, PD, R]

541. Siebert, Roger David. A history of the Shoshoni Indians of Wyoming. M.A.
     thesis (American Studies), University of Wyoming. Laramie, WY, 1961. vi +
     129 pp. [EH, IR, NA, PD]

542. Sievers, Michael A. Sands of Sand Creek historiography. The Colorado Maga-
     zine 49:116-142 (1972). [EH, IR]

543. Sifton, Rev. J. B. Pope Inibat. Prayers in the Arapahoe language. 1908.
     [1 p.] [L, R]

544. Sifton, Rev. J. B. Miscellaneous notes on the Arapaho language. [n.d.]
     [41 pp.] Manuscript. [L]

545. Simons, LaWanna. Northern Arapahoe--my people. Wambidiota News 5:10:5
     (November 7, 1986). Durango, CO: Ft. Lewis College. [MG, NA]

546. Sioux treaty of 1868. The Indian Historian 3:1:13-17 (1970). [TL]

547. Slotkin, J. S. The peyote religion: a study in Indian-white relations.
     Glencoe, IL: The Free Press, 1956. [IR, R]

548. Smet, P. J. de. Western missions and missionaries: a series of letters. New
     York, NY: P. J. Kenedy, 1860[?]. [EH]

549. Smith, Bruce. Wildlife and its management on the Wind River Indian Reserva-
     tion. Wyoming Wildlife 46:3:26-31 (March 1982). [NA, PD, RE]

550. Smith, Clarence. Legend of the Big Dipper. The Indian Craftsman 1:2:16-17
     (March 1909). Carlisle, PA. [OF]

551. Smith, Maurice Greer. Political organization of the Plains Indians, with
     special reference to the council. The University Studies of the University
     of Nebraska, Vol. 24, Part 1-2, pp. 1-84 (1925). [PS]

552. Snow, Riley E. Removal of the Indians from Wyoming. M.A. thesis (Political
      Science), Colorado State College of Education. Greeley, CO, 1936. x +
      211 pp. [EH, MG, NA, TL]

553. Snyder, Karen. Native American clothing. Ethete, WY: Wyoming Indian High
      School, 1985. 48 pp. [DA, IM, MC, PD]

554. Socolofsky, Homer E., and Huber Self. Historical atlas of Kansas. Norman, OK:
      University of Oklahoma Press, 1972. [EH]

555. The Southern Arapaho. U. S. Department of the Interior: Indian Arts and
      Crafts Board, Southern Plains Indian Museum and Crafts Center. [n.d.]
      [5 pp.] [MG, PD, SA]

556. Spier, Leslie. The sun dance of the Plains Indians: its development and dif-
      fusion. Anthropological Papers of the American Museum of Natural History
      16:7:451-527. New York, NY, 1921. [EH, IR, R]

557. Spoonhunter, Bob. Northern snows to southern summers; story based on legends
      told by Northern Arapaho elders. [An Arapaho odyssey.] Saint Stephens, WY:
      Saint Stephens Indian School, 1978. [14 pp.] [EH, F, IM, NA, OF, PD]

558. Spoonhunter, Bob, ed. Fast Runner. Saint Stephens, WY: Saint Stephens Indian
      School, 1978. [18 pp.] [IM, OF, PD]

559. Spoonhunter, Bob. The buffalo hunt. Saint Stephens, WY: Saint Stephens
      Indian School, 1978. 20 pp. [IM, NA, PD, S]

560. Spoonhunter, Bob. The Arapaho nation of Wind River. Saint Stephens, WY:
      Saint Stephens Indian School, 1978. [6 pp.] [EH, IM, IR, MG, NA]

561. Spoonhunter, Bob, ed. Counting my feathers. Saint Stephens, WY: Saint
      Stephens Indian School, 1978. [20 pp.] [F, IM, PD]

562. Spoonhunter, Bob. Peter Prairie Dog. Saint Stephens, WY: Saint Stephens
      Indian School, 1978. 24 pp. [IM, OF, PD]

563. Spoonhunter, Bob. Saint Stephens Indian School. Saint Stephens, WY: Saint
      Stephens Indian School, 1978. 16 pp. [ME, PD, R]

564. Spoonhunter, Bob. Arapaho games. Saint Stephens, WY: Saint Stephens Indian
      School, 1978. 9 pp. [G, IM, MC, PD]

565. Spoonhunter, Bob, ed. The girl and the porcupine. Saint Stephens, WY: Saint
      Stephens Indian School, 1979. [18 pp.] [IM, OF, PD]

566. Spoonhunter, Bob. Arapaho tipi. Saint Stephens, WY: Saint Stephens Indian
      School, 1979. [16 pp.] [IM, MC, PD]

567. Spoonhunter, Bob, ed. Fast Runner. Saint Stephens, WY: Saint Stephens Indian
      School, 1979. [18 pp.] [IM, OF, PD]

568. Spoonhunter, Bob. Arapaho values. Saint Stephens, WY: Saint Stephens Indian
      School, 1979. [15 pp.] [IM, PD, V]

569. Spoonhunter, Bob. Arapaho clothing. Saint Stephens, WY: Saint Stephens Indian
      School, 1979. 13 pp. [DA, IM, MC, PD]

570. Spoonhunter, Bob. Arapaho designs and symbols. Ethete, WY: Wyoming Indian
      High School, 1983. [19 pp.] [DA, IM, MC, PD]

571. Spoonhunter, Bob, ed. Arapaho legends. Ethete, WY: Wyoming Indian High
      School, 1983. [44 pp.] [IM, OF, PD]

572. Spoonhunter, Bob, and Martha Woodenlegs. [The] Arapahos on the Great Plains.
      Student workbook. Ethete, WY: Wyoming Indian High School, 1982. [22 pp.]
      [EH, IM, MC, MG, NA, PD, PS]

573. Spoonhunter, Bob, and others. Arapaho memories. Ethete, WY: Wyoming Indian High School, 1985. vi + 45 pp. [CC, EH, NA, PD]

574. Spoonhunter, James and Marguerite, trans. Animals and birds--Cise'hiiho' no' nii'ehiiho'. Saint Stephens, WY: Saint Stephens Indian School, 1979. [15 pp.] [IM, L, PD]

575. Stanley, Henry M. My early travels and adventures in America and Asia. Vol. 1. New York, NY: Charles Scribner's Sons, 1895. xxi + 301 pp. [EH]

576. Starkloff, Carl F. American Indian religion and Christianity: confrontation and dialog. Journal of Ecumenical Studies 8:317-340 (1971). [CC, NA, OF, R, V]

577. Starkloff, Carl F. American Indian religion and Christianity: confrontation and dialogue. In New Theology No. 9. Martin E. Marty and Dean G. Peerman, eds. Pp. 121-150. New York, NY: The Macmillan Company, 1972. [CC, NA, OF, R, V]

578. Starkloff, Carl F. The people of the center; American Indian religion and Christianity. New York, NY: The Seabury Press, 1974. 144 pp. [CC, NA, OF, R, V]

579. Starkloff, Carl F. Mission method and the American Indian. Theological Studies 38:4:621-653 (1977). [CC, NA, R]

580. Starkloff, Carl F. Cultural problems in mission catechesis among the Native Americans. Occasional Bulletin of Missionary Research 3:4:138-140 (October 1979). Ventnor, NJ: Overseas Ministries Study Center. [NA, R, V]

581. [Starkloff, Carl F.] Arapaho participation at the Tekakwitha Conference. The Wind River Rendezvous 13:3:14-15 (July-September 1983). Saint Stephens, WY: St. Stephen's Indian Mission Foundation. [NA, PD, R]

582. Starkloff, Carl F. Religious renewal in native North America: the contemporary call to mission. Missiology: An International Review 13:81-101 (1985). [CC, NA, R, V]

583. The start of the rainbow: the Wyoming Indian High School. Gulf Oilmanac 45:2:2-7 (February 1976). Pittsburgh, PA: Gulf Oil Corporation. [CA, ME, NA]

584. Status of lands withdrawn from Wind River Reservation for Riverton Reclamation Project[,] Wyoming. Billings, MT: Department of the Interior, Bureau of Indian Affairs, Missouri River Basin Investigations, Report No. 76. 1949. [Mimeographed.] 29 pp. + append. and exhibits. [CA, NA, RE]

585. Stearns, Robert L. Who have the power? The Colorado Magazine 16:1-13 (1939). [EH, TL]

586. Stenberg, Molly Peacock. The peyote cult among Wyoming Indians; a transitional link between an indigenous culture and an imposed culture. M.A. thesis (Economics and Sociology), University of Wyoming. Laramie, WY, 1945. xii + 185 pp. [CC, IR, NA, PD, R]

587. Stenberg, Molly Peacock. The peyote culture among Wyoming Indians; a transitional link between an indigenous culture and an imposed culture. University of Wyoming Publications, Vol. 12, No. 4, pp. 85-156 (1946). [CC, IR, NA, PD, R]

588. Stewart, Donald D. Cheyenne-Arapaho assimilation. Phylon 13:120-126 (1952). Atlanta, GA. [CC, EH, IR, SA]

589. Stewart, Frank Henderson. Fundamentals of age-group systems. New York, NY: Academic Press, 1977. xv + 381 pp. [PS]

590. Stewart, Omer C. The peyote religion and the ghost dance. The Indian Historian 5:4:27-30 (1972). [IR, R]

591. Stoller, Marianne L. A sacred bundle of the Arapaho Indians. Annals of
     Carnegie Museum 35:11-25 (1957). Pittsburgh, PA. [MC, PD, R, SA]

592. Stoll-Sage, Barbara. Tribal government at Wind River; the modern era. Ethete,
     WY: Wyoming Indian High School, [1985]. iii + 14 + iv-ix pp. [CC, EH, IR,
     NA, PD, PS]

593. Stone, Forrest R. Indians at work and play; a series of three articles de-
     scribing Shoshone reservation activities. [n.d.] 10 pp. [Mimeographed.]
     [IR, ME, MG, NA, RE]

594. The story of Francis.... The Wind River Rendezvous 7:3:2-8 (May-June 1977).
     Saint Stephens, WY: Saint Stephens Indian Mission. [LH, NA]

595. Story teller. The Wind River Rendezvous 9:5:4-6 (September-October 1979).
     Saint Stephens, WY: Saint Stephens Indian Mission. [CA, NA, OF, PD]

596. Stuart, Robert. The discovery of the Oregon Trail; Robert Stuart's narratives
     of his overland trip eastward from Astoria in 1812-13. New York, NY: Charles
     Scribner's Sons, 1935. cxxxvii + 391 pp. [EH, MG]

597. Sutter, Virginia. Today's strength from yesterday's tradition--the continuity
     of the American Indian woman. Listening Post (A Periodical of the Mental
     Health Programs, Indian Health Service) 4:2:3-13 (April 1982). [Albuquerque,
     NM.] [CA, CC, MG]

598. Sutter, Virginia. Today's strength from yesterday's tradition--the continuity
     of the American Indian woman. Frontiers: A Journal of Women Studies 6:3:53-57
     (1982). Boulder, CO. [CA, CC, MG]

599. Swanson, Evadene Burris. Friday: roving Arapaho. Annals of Wyoming 47:59-68
     (1975). [EH, LH, NA, PD]

600. Sweezy, Carl [as told to Althea Bass]. A long way from the buffalo road.
     American Heritage 17:6:22-25, 92-98 (October 1966). [EH, MG, PD, SA]

601. Swindell, Jemna L. An ex-post-facto study of the differences in the visually
     artistic sensibilities between Indian and non-Indian children in elementary
     schools on the Wind River Reservation. M.A. thesis (Curriculum and Instruc-
     tion), University of Wyoming. Laramie, WY, 1977. vi + 61 pp. [DA, ME, NA,
     P]

602. Talbot, Theodore. The journals of Theodore Talbot, 1843 and 1849-52; with the
     Fremont expedition of 1843 and with the first military company in Oregon
     Territory, 1849-1852. Edited, with notes, by Charles H. Carey. Portland,
     OR: Metropolitan Press, 1931. x + 153 pp. [EH]

603. Tallman, Elizabeth J. Pioneer experiences in Colorado. The Colorado Magazine
     13:141-149 (1936). [Interviewed by James R. Harvey.] [EH, PD]

604. Taylor, Allan R. Some observations on a comparative Arapaho-Atsina lexicon.
     National Museum of Canada, Bulletin No. 214, Anthropological Series No. 78,
     Contributions to Anthropology: Linguistics I (Algonquian). Pp. 113-127.
     Ottawa, 1967. [L, NA]

605. Taylor, Morris F. Some aspects of historical Indian occupation of southeastern
     Colorado. Great Plains Journal 4:17-28 (1964). [EH]

606. Tefft, Stanton K. Anomy, values and culture change among teen-age Indians: an
     exploratory study. Sociology of Education 40:145-15, (1967). [CC, ME, NA,
     V]

607. Tefft, Stanton K. Task experience and intertribal value differences on the
     Wind River Reservation. Social Forces 49:604-614 (1971). [IR, P, V]

608. Thayer, B. W. Additional Arapaho moccasin characteristics. The Minnesota
     Archaeologist 8:2:[30-]31-40 (April 1942). [DA, MC]

609. Thomas, Nathaniel S. Historical sketch of the Church in Wyoming. (Convo-
     cational sermon.) [1918?]. 37 pp. [NA, R]

610. Thomas, Nathaniel S. St. Michael's Mission project[,] Ethete, Wyoming; the
     background of an interesting endeavor to solve the Indian problem of re-
     versal to type. [1924?]. 16 pp. [ME, NA, PD, R]

611. Thompson, David. David Thompson's narrative, 1784-1812. Edited by Richard
     Glover. The Publications of the Champlain Society XL. Toronto, 1962. [EH]

612. Thompson, Stith. The Star Husband tale. Studia Septentrionalia 4:93-163
     (1953). Oslo. [OF, PD]

613. Thunder, Debbie. Women of the Blue Sky. Wind River Cache 1:1:21-24 (January
     1982). Lander, WY. [CC, EH, LH, NA, PD]

614. Thunder, Debbie. "Beautiful traditions." Wind River Cache 1:2:45-48 (May
     1982). Lander, WY. [CC, EH, LH, NA, PD]

615. Thwaites, Reuben Gold, ed. Early Western Travels[,] 1748-1846; a series of
     annotated reprints of some of the best and rarest contemporary volumes of
     travel, descriptive of the aborigines and social and economic conditions in
     the Middle and Far West, during the period of early American settlement.
     Volume XVI, Part III of James's account of S. H. Long's Expedition, 1819-
     1820. Cleveland, OH: The Arthur H. Clark Company, 1905. 291 pp. [EH, MG,
     PD]

616. Tierney, Luke, William B. Parsons, and others. Pike's Peak gold rush guide-
     books of 1859. Ed. by LeRoy R. Hafen. (The Southwest Historical Series IX.)
     Glendale, CA: The Arthur H. Clark Company, 1941. 346 pp. + map. [EH]

617. Toll, Oliver W. Arapaho names and trails; a report of a 1914 pack trip. 1962.
     43 pp. [EH, L, PD]

618. Townsend, Charles Vernard. The opening of the Cheyenne and Arapahoe country.
     M.A. thesis (History), Oklahoma Agricultural and Mechanical College. Still-
     water, OK, 1939. iv + 55 pp. [CC, EH, IR, SA, TL]

619. A treaty despoiled; the story of the Fort Reno military lands. [1952?]. 17 pp.
     [EH, NA, SA, TL]

620. Treaty of 1868. Saint Stephens, WY: Saint Stephens Indian School, 1978. [4 pp.]
     [EH, IM, NA, TL]

621. Treaty of 1863. Saint Stephens, WY: Saint Stephens Indian School, 1978. [4 pp.]
     [EH, IM, NA, TL]

622. Trenholm, Virginia Cole. The Arapahoes, our people. (The Civilization of the
     American Indian Series, Vol. 105.) Norman, OK: University of Oklahoma Press,
     1970. xviii + 373 pp. [EH, IR, MG, PD]

623. Trenholm, Virginia Cole. Arapahoes in council. Annals of Wyoming 44:234-236
     (1972). [EH, MG, PD]

624. Trenholm, Virginia Cole. Amanda Mary and the Dog Soldiers. Annals of Wyoming
     46:5-46 (1974). [EH, NA]

625. Trenholm, Virginia Cole, and Maurine Carley. Wyoming pageant. Casper, WY:
     Prairie Publishing Company, 1946. 272 pp. [EH, IR, MG, NA, PD]

626. Trenholm, Virginia Cole, and Maurine Carley. The Shoshonis; sentinels of the
     Rockies. Norman, OK: University of Oklahoma Press, 1964. xiii + 367 pp.
     [EH, IR, NA, PD]

627. Tribal council[,] a lot of responsibility. Wind River Rendezvous 2:6:5 (Novem-
     ber-December 1972). Saint Stephens, WY: Saint Stephens Indian School. [BE,
     LH, NA, PD, PS]

628. The tribe's "Man Friday." Wind River Rendezvous 2:4:1-2 (July-August 1972).
      Saint Stephens, WY: Saint Stephens Indian School. [BE, CC, LH, MG, NA, PD]

629. Tyler, Barrett P. First families of Wyoming; St. Michael's Mission to the
      Arapahoe Indians, at Ethete, Wyoming. 1935. 19 pp. [Printed in The
      Cathedral Quarterly for January 1935.] [MG, NA, R]

630. Uhlenbeck, C. C. Additional Blackfoot-Arapaho comparisons. International
      Journal of American Linguistics 4:227-228 (1927). [L]

631. Underhill, Ruth M. Peyote. Proceedings of the Thirtieth International Con-
      gress of Americanists: Cambridge 1952. 1955. Pp. 143-148. [R, SA]

632. Underhill, Ruth, and students. Modern Arapaho. Southwestern Lore 17:2:38-42
      (1951). [CC, LH, MG, SA]

633. Unrau, William Errol. The role of the Indian agent in the settlement of the
      south-central Plains, 1861-1868. Dissertation Abstracts, Vol. XXV, Part 3,
      p. 1884 (September 1964). [EH, IR, SA]

634. Unrau, William E. A prelude to war. The Colorado Magazine 41:299-313 (1964).
      [EH, IR, PD]

635. Vanderwerth, W. C., comp. Indian oratory: famous speeches by noted Indian
      chieftains. (The Civilization of the American Indian Series, Vol. 110.)
      Norman, OK: University of Oklahoma Press, 1971. xviii + 292 pp. [Little
      Raven, pp. 138-144.] [LH, PD, TL]

636. Venite, exultemus Domino. [n.d.]. [2 pp.]. [L, R]

637. Vestal, Stanley. Kit Carson, the happy warrior of the Old West; a biography.
      Boston, MA: Houghton Mifflin, 1928. xii + 297 pp. [EH, LH, MG, SA]

638. Vestal, Stanley. 'Dobe walls; a story of Kit Carson's Southwest. Boston, MA:
      Houghton Mifflin Company, 1929. [v] + 314 pp. [EH, F]

639. Videbeck, Richard. Review of M. Inez Hilger, Arapaho child life and its cul-
      tural background. The Plains Anthropologist, No. 5, 1955, pp. 37-38.

640. Voegelin, C. F. Sign language analysis, on one level or two? International
      Journal of American Linguistics 24:71-77 (1958). [L, NA]

641. Vogdes, Ada A. The journal of Ada A. Vogdes, 1868-71. Edited by Donald K.
      Adams. Montana, the Magazine of Western History 13:3:2-17 (1963). [MG, NA,
      PD]

642. Vogel, Virgil J. This country was ours: a documentary history of the American
      Indian. New York, NY: Harper and Row, 1972. xxx + 473 pp. [EH, OF, TL]

643. Voth, H. R. Funeral customs among the Cheyenne and Arapahoe Indians. The
      Folk-Lorist, Journal of the Chicago Folk-Lore Society 1:95-98 (1893). [R]

644. Voth, H. R. Arapaho tales. Journal of American Folk-lore 25:43-50 (1912).
      [OF]

645. Vrettos, Louis. The education of Indians with special reference to the Sho-
      shone Indian reservation in Wyoming. M.A. thesis (Education), University of
      Wyoming. Laramie, WY, 1949. vi + 54 pp. [ME, MG, NA]

646. Wagner, Marsden G., and Bruce Littman. Phenylketonuria in the American Indian.
      Pediatrics 39:108-110 (1967). [MB, SA]

647. Wake, C. Staniland. Traits of an ancient Egyptian folk-tale, compared with
      those of aboriginal American tales. The Journal of American Folk-Lore 17:
      255-264 (1904). [OF]

648. Wake, C. Staniland. Nihancan, the white man. The American Antiquarian and Oriental Journal 26:225-231 (1904). [OF]

649. Wake, C. Staniland. Mythology of the Plains' Indians. The American Antiquarian and Oriental Journal 27:9-16, 73-78, 323-328 (1905). [OF]

650. Wake, C. Staniland. Asiatic ideas among the American Indians. The American Antiquarian and Oriental Journal 27:153-162, 189-197 (1905). [OF]

651. Waldman, Carl. Atlas of the North American Indian. New York, NY: Facts on File Publications, 1985. xi + 276 pp. [EH, MG, PD]

652. Walker, Tacetta B. Stories of early days in Wyoming: Big Horn Basin. Casper, WY: Prairie Publishing Company, 1936. vi + 271 pp. [EH, MG, NA]

653. Warner, Mildred. The attitude of the Nebraska territorial government towards the Indians: II. Great Plains Journal 9:59-66 (1970). [EH, TL]

654. The way it was. The Wind River Rendezvous 1:2:5 (March-April 1971). Saint Stephens, WY: Saint Stephens Indian Mission. [CC, LH, NA]

655. Webb, Frances Seely. The Indian version of the Platte Bridge fight. Annals of Wyoming 32:234-236 (1960). [EH, IR, NA]

656. Wedel, Waldo R. An introduction to Kansas archaeology. Smithsonian Institution, Bureau of American Ethnology, Bulletin 174, pp. 80-81. Washington, DC: GPO, 1959. [EH]

657. Weist, Katherine M., and Susan R. Sharrock. An annotated bibliography of Northern Plains ethnohistory. Contributions to Anthropology, No. 8. Missoula, MT: Department of Anthropology, University of Montana, 1985. 299 pp. [B]

658. Wells, Betty L. Political socialization of Indian and white children in Wyoming. M.A. thesis (Sociology), University of Wyoming. Laramie, WY, 1974. v + 93 pp. [ME, NA, P, PS]

659. Welsh, Peter Hamilton. "Taking care of your own": identity and dependency among the Northern Arapahoe. Ph.D. dissertation (Anthropology), University of Pennsylvania. Philadelphia, PA, 1986. xi + 332 pp. [BE, CA, CC, EH, MC, MG, NA, PS, RE, S, TL, V]

660. West, La Mont. The sign language, an analysis. Ph.D. dissertation (Anthropology), Indiana University. Bloomington, IN, 1960. Vol. I, pp. 1-128; Vol. II, pp. 1-170. [L, NA]

661. Wheeler, Homer W. Reminiscences of old Fort Washakie. State of Wyoming Historical Department Quarterly Bulletin 1:4:1-4 (1924). [EH, NA]

662. Where the cowboys are Indians. The Wind River Rendezvous 11:5:3-6 (September-October 1981). Saint Stephens, WY: Saint Stephens Indian Mission. [BE, CA, NA, PD]

663. White, Lonnie J. The Cheyenne barrier on the Kansas frontier, 1868-1869. Arizona and the West 4:51-64 (1962). [EH, SA]

664. White, Lonnie J. The Hancock and Custer expeditions of 1867. Journal of the West 5:355-378 (1966). [EH, IR]

665. [Whitehawk, Michael, trans.] Hethadenee Waunauyaunee Vadan Luke Vanenāna. The Gospel according to Saint Luke. New York, NY: American Bible Society, 1903. 102 pp. [L, R]

666. Whiteman, Henrietta. Cheyenne-Arapaho education, 1871-1982. Ph.D. dissertation (American Studies), University of New Mexico. Alguquerque, NM, 1982. xii + 318 pp. [CC, IR, ME, MG, SA]

667. Wildschut, William. Arapaho medicine bundle. Indian Notes 4:83-88 (1927).
      [MB, MC, NA, R]

668. Wildschut, William. Arapaho medicine-mirror. Indian Notes 4:252-257 (1927).
      [MB, MC, NA, PD, R]

669. Wildschut, William. Arapaho medicine bundle. The American Indian 2:4:12-13
      (January 1928). Tulsa. [MB, MC, NA, R]

670. Wildschut, William. Arapaho medicine mirror. The American Indian 2:4:14
      (January 1928). Tulsa. [MB, MC, NA, R]

671. Will, George F., and George E. Hyde. Corn among the Indians of the Upper
      Missouri. Saint Louis, MO: The William Harvey Miner Company, 1917. 323 pp.
      [EH, MG, OF, PD, S]

672. William Shakespeare--"Strikes again." The Wind River Rendezvous 4:2:1-3
      (March-April 1974). Saint Stephens, WY: Saint Stephens Indian Mission.
      [LH, NA, PD]

673. Williams, Gerald. The Colorado Indian problem, 1858-1876. M.A. thesis,
      University of Oklahoma. Norman, OK, 1936. xxiv + 89 pp. [EH, IR]

674. Willow, Joan. Arapaho names. Ethete, WY: Wyoming Indian High School, 1984.
      16 pp. [CC, IM, K, MG, NA, PD]

675. Willow, V. James, comp. Winter counts, symbols, and pictographs. Ethete, WY:
      Wyoming Indian High School, [n.d.]. [31 pp.] [EH, IM, MC, PD]

676. Willow, V. James, comp. Shield art. Ethete, WY: Wyoming Indian High School,
      [1983?]. 28 pp. [DA, F, IM, MC, MG, PD, R]

677. Wilson, H. L. The trail of the Arapaho nation. [n.d.]. 3 pp. [EH, MG, NA]

678. Wilson, Paul B. Farming and ranching on the Wind River Indian Reservation,
      Wyoming. Ph.D. dissertation (Geography), University of Nebraska. Lincoln,
      NE, 1972. vi + 433 pp. [BE, CA, CC, EH, IR, MC, MG, NA, RE]

679. Wilson, Paul Burns. Farming and ranching on the Wind River Indian Reservation,
      Wyoming. Dissertation Abstracts International: B--The Sciences and En-
      gineering, Vol. 34, Part I, pp. 272-B-273-B (July 1973). [NA, RE]

680. Wilson, Terry Paul. Panaceas for progress: efforts to educate the Southern
      Cheyennes and Arapahoes, 1870-1908. M.A. thesis (History), University of
      Oklahoma. Norman, OK, 1965. iv + 104 pp. [CC, IR, ME, R, SA]

681. Wind River Indian Reservation. Saint Stephens, WY: Saint Stephens Indian
      School, 1978. [4 pp.] [IM, MG, NA]

682. [Map of the] Wind River Indian Reservation. Highway system map: Wind River
      Indian Agency. U.S. Department of the Interior, Bureau of Indian Affairs,
      Billings Area Office, Branch of Roads. 1975, revised 1985. 6 sheets.
      1 inch = 2 miles. [NA]

683. The Wind River Reservation yesterday and today: the legends--the land--the
      people. [n.d.]. 58 pp. [ME, MG, NA, PS, TL]

684. Wissler, Clark. Costumes of the Plains Indians. Anthropological Papers of
      the American Museum of Natural History 17:2:39-91 (1915). New York, NY.
      [DA, IR, MC]

685. Wissler, Clark. Structural basis to the decoration of costumes among the
      Plains Indians. Anthropological Papers of the American Museum of Natural
      History 17:3:93-114 (1916). New York, NY. [DA, IR, MC]

686. Wissler, Clark. Moccasin exhibit in the American Museum. The American Museum
      Journal 16:308-314 (1916). New York, NY. [DA, MC, PD]

687. Wissler, Clark. Distribution of moccasin decorations among the Plains tribes.
      Anthropological Papers of the American Museum of Natural History 29:1:1-23
      (1927). New York, NY. [DA, IR, MC, PD]

688. Wissler, Clark. Indians of the United States; four centuries of their history
      and culture. Garden City, NY: Doubleday[, Doran] and Company, 1940, 1944.
      xvi + 319 pp. [MG]

689. Wissler, Clark. North American Indians of the Plains. American Museum of
      Natural History, Handbook Series No. 1. New York, NY, 1948. 172 pp. [MG,
      PD]

690. Wissler, Clark. Indians of the United States. Revised edition [by Lucy W.
      Kluckhohn]. Garden City, NY: Doubleday and Company, 1966. 336 pp. [MG]

691. Wood, W. Raymond, and Margot Liberty, eds. Anthropology on the Great Plains.
      Lincoln, NE: University of Nebraska Press, 1980. vii + 306 pp. [CC, DA,
      EH, H, K, L, M, MG, PS, R]

692. Wooden Legs, Martha. Fast Moccasin; a story of Arapaho kinship. [Student
      workbook.] Ethete, WY: Wyoming Indian High School, 1983. [25 pp.] [F, IM,
      K, MG, NA, PD]

693. Woodward, George A. The Northern Cheyenne at Fort Fetterman; Colonel Woodward
      describes some experiences of 1871. Montana, the Magazine of Western His-
      tory 9:2:16-27 (1959). [EH, NA]

694. Wright, Muriel H. A guide to the Indian tribes of Oklahoma. Norman, OK:
      University of Oklahoma Press, 1951. [MG, PD, SA]

695. Wright, Patricia. New life for a dying language; Arapaho children use video
      technology to learn Arapaho. Contact; University of Massachusetts at Am-
      herst 11:2:16-19 (Winter 1986). [CA, L, ME, NA, PD]

696. Wright, Peter Melton. Fort Reno, Indian Territory, 1874-1885. M.A. thesis
      (History), University of Oklahoma. Norman, OK, 1965. xi + 119 pp. [EH,
      PD, SA]

697. Wyoming Indians. 63 pp. [1944]. [CC, NA, PD, R]

                                    Addenda

698. Hafen, Le Roy R. Broken Hand: the life of Thomas Fitzpatrick:[,] mountain
      man, guide and [&] Indian agent. Rev. ed. Denver, CO: Old West Publishing
      Company, 1973. xiii + 359 pp. Lincoln, NE: University of Nebraska Press,
      1981. xiv + 359 pp. [LH, NA]

699. Parkman, Francis. The Oregon trail: sketches of prairie and Rocky-mountain
      life. Boston: Little, Brown, and Company, 1892. xx + 411 pp. (The work
      was serialized in Knickerbocker Magazine, Vols. 29-33 [February 1847-
      February 1849] and appeared in a number of editions.) [EH, IR, PD]

700. Schöppl von Sonnwalden, Herman. Rang, Führerschaft und soziale Wertschätzung
      bei den Cheyenne und Arapaho. Wyk auf Föhr, West Germany: Verlag für
      Amerikanistik D. Kuegler, 1986. 119 pp. [PD, PS, V]

701. Shields, Lillian B. The Arapaho Indians, their association with the White man.
      M.A. thesis, University of Denver. Denver, CO, 1929. 72 pp. [EH, IR]

702. Voegelin, Erminie Wheeler. Mythological elements common to the Kiowa and five
      other Plains tribes. M.A. thesis (Anthropology), University of California.
      Berkeley, CA, 1932. 55 pp. [OF]

Topical Index to the Bibliography

Pictorial documentation (cont.): 557-559, 561-574, 581, 586, 587, 591, 592, 595, 599, 600, 603, 610, 612-615, 617, 622, 623, 625-628, 634, 635, 641, 651, 662, 668, 671, 672, 674-676, 686, 687, 689, 692, 694-697, 699, 700

Political/social organization: 42, 100, 101, 130, 142, 161, 173, 186, 189-192, 249, 266, 285, 312, 313, 317, 335, 336, 348, 351, 399, 401, 422, 426, 533, 551, 572, 589, 592, 627, 658, 659, 683, 691, 700

Psychology: 92, 93, 112, 182, 183, 185, 272, 273, 335, 336, 357, 364, 401, 435, 480, 601, 607, 658

Religion: 1, 6, 11, 23, 28, 30, 35, 36, 40, 42, 45, 57, 63, 78, 79, 81, 110, 121, 125, 130, 135, 136, 157, 199, 213, 224, 249, 251, 253, 255, 265, 266, 279-281, 283, 300-303, 309, 312-314, 317, 325, 334, 342, 348, 350, 351, 377, 381, 392, 396, 405, 408, 423, 429, 430, 433, 439, 459, 470, 473, 517-521, 523, 533, 537, 539, 540, 543, 547, 556, 563, 576-582, 586, 587, 590, 591, 609, 610, 629, 631, 636, 643, 665, 667-670, 676, 680, 691, 697

Reservation ecology: 3, 28, 34, 48, 52, 80, 111, 119, 120, 141, 187, 233, 271, 278, 434, 456, 460, 526, 528, 529, 536, 549, 584, 593, 659, 678, 679

Southern Arapaho (primarily or exclusively): 1, 9, 20, 28, 39-41, 44, 46-50, 52, 53, 67, 72, 79, 83, 95, 97, 98, 101, 111, 119, 120, 124, 125, 128, 130, 134, 140, 142-144, 149, 153-159, 161, 193, 200, 215, 216, 233, 248, 263, 288, 290, 291, 296, 299, 301, 303, 305, 308, 309, 318, 338, 348, 363, 368, 370, 371, 379, 388, 390, 391, 427, 430, 433-435, 442, 459, 460, 464, 466, 473, 474, 514, 515, 528- 531, 555, 588, 591, 600, 618, 619, 631-633, 637, 646, 663, 666, 680, 694, 696

Subsistence: 19, 42, 65, 67, 191, 266, 312, 317, 426, 434, 515, 559, 659, 671

Treaties/legal affairs: 9, 11, 20, 37, 46, 47, 50, 53, 56, 89, 90, 96, 99-101, 111, 118, 119, 134, 144, 149, 159, 161-165, 167, 189, 200, 215, 216, 227, 229, 233, 239, 240, 242, 244, 271, 278, 289, 292, 295, 298, 304, 318, 321, 327, 356, 359, 403, 404, 424, 427, 460, 466, 467, 476, 525, 528, 529, 534, 546, 552, 585, 618- 621, 635, 642, 653, 659, 683

Values: 89, 90, 112, 136, 172, 174, 175, 177-179, 181, 182, 184, 224, 230-232, 255, 266, 272, 273, 326, 334-336, 364, 401, 435, 484, 568, 576-578, 580, 582, 606, 607, 659, 700

The following entries refer to reviews: 51, 82, 170, 226, 340, 384, 639

The Arapaho Indians in the
Public Documents of the
United States

A

Guide to American Indian Documents in the Congressional Serial Set: 1817–1899

by STEVEN L. JOHNSON

The following entries pertaining to the Arapaho Indians have been derived from Steven L. Johnson's Guide to American Indian Documents in the Congressional Serial Set: 1817-1899 (New York, NY: Clearwater Publishing Company, © 1977). Permission to reprint the material below, copyrighted by Clearwater Publishing Company, Inc., 1995 Broadway, New York, NY 10023, is hereby gratefully acknowledged. The Guide is confined to those documents and reports that were ordered to be printed by the 15th through the 55th Congresses, that is, during the period between December 1, 1817, and March 3, 1899, and published in the Congressional Serial Set.

Each entry consists of document title and date, document citation, and brief description of the contents of the document. The document citation includes reference to the document series (e.g., HR), the document number (e.g., 208), number of the Congress and session (e.g., 19-1), the volume in which the document is printed (e.g., v2), the number of pages in the document (e.g., 1p.), and in brackets the serial number of the volume in which the document is to be found (e.g., [142]). Thus, "HR 208, 19-1, v2, 1p. [142]" is to be read in full as "House Report number 208, 19th Congress, 1st session, volume 2, 1 page, Serial Set volume number 142."

The entries are arranged chronologically by year, and within each year according to the Serial Set number and date; they are reprinted exactly as they appear in the Guide.

The following abbreviations are used:

Capt.	Captain
CIA	Commissioner of Indian Affairs
Co.	Company
Col.	Colonel
com'r	commissioner
Dept.	Department
Gen.	General
HD	House Document
HED	House Executive Document
HMD	House Miscellaneous Document
HR	House Report
L-C	Letter on the claim
Legis.	Legislature
Maj.	Major
Mem.	Memorial
p.	page(s)
Pres.	President
pt.	part
R-C	Report on the claim
Rep.	Representative
Resol.	Resolution

R-M   Report on the memorial
R-P   Report on the petition
SD   Senate Document
Sec.   Secretary
SED   Senate Executive Document
Sen.   Senator
SMD   Senate Miscellaneous Document
SR   Senate Report
Supt.   Superintendent
U.S.   United States
v   volume

1826   R-C of B. and A. Smith. 12 May.
        HR 208, 19-1, v2, 1p. [142]
        Cattle taken by Arapaho Indians near Santa Fe.

1836   Journal of Col. Dodge's Expedition. 23 Feb.
        SD 209, 24-1, v3, 38p. [281] or HD 181, 24-1, v4, 38p. [289]
        To the Rocky Mountains in 1835; talks with the Ottoe, Omaha, Pawnee, Arikara,
        Cheyenne, Arapaho, Gros Ventre, and Blackfoot Indians; maps.

1848   Communication on Indians in Texas. 15 June.
        SR 171, 30-1, v1, 52p. [512]
        Relations with said Indians; depredations by the Comanches, Arapahoes, Kiowas,
        and other tribes of the Southwest; treaty negotiations.

1856   R-P of J. Hall. 2 Aug.
        HR 299, 34-1, v3, 4p. [870]
        Independence-Santa Fe mail route; Pawnee, Cheyenne, Comanche, Apache, Kiowa,
        and Arrapahoe hostilities.

1859   R-P of W. Bent. 1 Feb.
        HR 151, 35-2, v1, 1p. [1018]
        Kiowa, Cheyenne, Arapahoe, and Apache depredations during 1854-1855.

1860   Report on Holding Treaty Councils with Indians. 16 Apr.
        SED 35, 36-1, v9, 19p. [1031] or HED 61, 36-1, v9, 19p. [1051]
        With the Kiowas, Comanches, and others on the Arkansas River; with the
        Arapahoes and Cheyennes on the Platte River; with the Sioux and others on
        Deer Creek; with the Red Lake Chippewas and others on the Red River of the
        north.

        Annual Message to Congress with Documents; Pres. Buchanan. 4 Dec.
        SED 1, 36-2, v1-3, 2130p. [1078-1080]
        Indian hostilities in Utah; annual report of the Sec. of War (Serial 1079);
        annual report of the Sec. of the Interior (Serial 1078); annual report of
        the General Land Office (Serial 1078), including intruders on Cherokee lands,
        commision to the Cheyennes and Arrapahoes, trust funds, and reports of Supts.,
        agents, and schools; etc.

1864   Appropriations for Indian Tribes. 19 Apr.
        HED 73, 38-1, v13, 2p. [1193]
        Appointment of an agent for the Kiowa, Apache, and Comanche Indians; at
        present they are under the charge of the Cheyenne-Arapaho agent.

1865   Report on Conduct of the War. 20 Feb.
        SR 142, 38-2, v2-4, 2318p. [1212-1214]
        Volume 3 (Serial 1214) contains testimony concerning the massacre of over
        100 Cheyenne and Arapahoe Indians at Sand Creek, Colorado Territory, by U.S.
        troops under Col. Chivington and Maj. Anthony.

        Annual Message to Congress with Documents; Pres. Johnson. 4 Dec.
        HED 1, 39-1, v1-6, 6827p. [1244-1254]
        Annual report of the Sec. of War (Serials 1249-1252); annual report of the
        Sec. of Interior (Serial 1248); annual report of the Gen. Land Office
        (Serial 1248); annual report of the CIA (Serial 1248), including trust lands,
        trust funds, populations, council proceedings with the Arapahoes, Cheyennes,
        Apaches, Kiowas, and Comanches, and reports of Supts., agents, and schools;
        etc.

1867   Report on the Sand Creek Massacre. 14 Feb.
        SED 26, 39-2, v2, 228p. [1277]
        Investigation of Col. Chivington's actions against the Cheyennes and
        Arapahoes in 1864.

        Letter on Com'rs to Indian Tribes. 14 Feb.
        HED 88, 39-2, v11, 5p. [1293]
        Funds for a commission to the Southwest, to visit Comanches, Kiowas, Cheyennes,
        Arapahoes, Lipans, Mescalaros, Kickapoos, and other Indians, in order to es-
        tablish peaceful relations with said tribes.

1867   Letter on Issue of Arms to Indians.   2 Feb.
        HMD 41, 39-2, v1, 4p. [1302]
        Sale of arms to Kiowas, Cheyennes, Sioux, Arapahoes, Comanches, and
        Apaches; possibility of war on the Kansas frontier.

        Letter on Indian Hostilities.   13 July.
        SED 13, 40-1, v1, 128p. [1308]
        Reports on conditions on the frontier; Fort Phil. Kearney massacre; sale of
        arms to Indians; Cheyennes, Arapahoes, and Sioux on the northern Plains;
        Cheyennes, Arapahoes, Comanches, and Kiowas on the southern plains.

1868   Survey of Lands for Cheyennes and Arapahoes.   16 Jan.
        HED 104, 40-2, v11, 12p. [1337]
        Half-breed lands under the treaty of 14 Oct. 1865; trouble may arise, as the
        Union Pacific Railroad will pass through the reserves.

        Subsistence of Indians.   26 May.
        HED 239, 40-2, v15, 3p. [1341]
        By the War Dept.; treaties signed with the Sioux, Crows, and Arapahoes.

        Indian Tribes in Kansas.   24 Apr.
        HED 263, 40-2, v17, 3p. [1343]
        Destitute condition of the Kaws, Quapaws, and Osages; these Indians warring
        with the Cheyennes, Arapahoes, and Apaches.

        Appropriations for Friendly Indians.   29 May.
        HED 296, 40-2, v19, 4p. [1345]
        Kawas, Osages, Apaches, Arapahoes, and Cheyennes; end of hostilities after
        the council at Medicine Lodge Creek.

1869   Battle of the Washita River.   7 Jan.
        SED 13, 40-3, v1, 38p. [1360]
        Between U.S. troops under Gen. Custer, and Cheyennes, Arapahoes, Kiowas, and
        Comanches; events leading up to the battle.

        Battle on the Washita River.   11 Jan.
        SED 18, 40-3, v1. 51p. [1360]
        Between U.S. troops under Gen. Custer, and Cheyennes, Arapahoes, Kiowas, and
        Comanches; 27 Nov. 1868; Indian war on the southern plains; events surround-
        ing the battle.

        Appropriations for the Cheyenne and Arapaho Indians.   19 Jan.
        SED 23, 40-3, v1, 8p. [1360]
        Under the treaty of 10 May 1868, made with them by the Indian Peace Com-
        mission at Fort Laramie, Dakota Territory.

        Indian Affairs in the Military Division of Missouri.   4 Feb.
        SED 40, 40-3, v1, 17p. [1360]
        Kiowa, Cheyenne, Arapaho, and Comanche hostilities; visit to the site of the
        battle of Washita.

        Resol. of the Kansas Legis.   1 Feb.
        SMD 32, 40-3, v1, 1p. [1361]
        Ask payment of claims against Arapaho, Cheyenne, Kiowa, and Comanche Indians
        for depredations during 1863-1864.

        Disbursements for Indian Tribes.   13 Dec.
        SED 5, 41-2, v1, 2p. [1405]
        For the maintenance of peace; excess expenditures of the Indian Peace Com-
        mission; subsistence for Sioux, Kiowas, Comanches, Apaches, Cheyennes, and
        Arapahoes; supplies for Plains Indians.

1870   Appropriations for Certain Indian Treaties.   8 Mar.
        SED 57, 41-2, v2, 5p. [1406]
        To carry out treaties made by the Indian Peace Commission; Indian hostilities
        arising because of nonfulfillment by U.S.; Piegans, Sioux, Utes, Cheyennes,
        Arapahoes, and other Plains Indians being forced into hostilities.

1870   Letter on Indian Tribes in the U.S.   29 Apr.
        SMD 136, 41-2, v1, 26p. [1408]
        List of tribes, their location, their population, and their condition; all
        tribes peaceable except for Blackfeet, Bloods, Piegans, Sioux, Cheyennes,
        Arapahoes, Kiowas, and Comanches.

        Establishment of Indian Tribes.   11 Feb.
        HED 125, 41-2, v6, 3p. [1417]
        Location and establishment of Kiowas, Comanches, Apaches, Arapahoes, Sacs,
        Foxes, and Cheyennes on lands in Indian Territory.

        Difficulties with Indian Tribes.   6 Apr.
        HED 240, 41-2, v11, 179p. [1425]
        With Cheyennes, Arapahoes, Comanches, Apaches, and Kiowas during 1867; em-
        ployment of Osages in the military service; attack on the Cheyenne village
        on the Washita.

        Appropriations for Indians.   11 May.
        HED 261, 41-2, v12, 2p. [1426]
        Subsistence for the Arapahoes, Cheyennes, Apaches, Kiowas, and Comanches;
        the failure of Congress to carry out treaty stipulations has prevented the
        placement of these Indians on reservations where they might grow crops.

        Education of Indians of the Central Superintendency.   20 May.
        HED 284, 41-2, v12, 3p. [1426]
        Appropriations required at the Kiowa and Comanche agency, and the Cheyenne
        and Arapaho agency.

        Appropriation to Pay Certain Indian Depredation Claims.   14 July.
        HED 311, 41-2, v13, 2p. [1427]
        Claims against the Cheyennes and Arapahoes.

        Papers on Indian Depredations.   10 Jan.
        HMD 20, 41-2, v1, 7p. [1431]
        Losses on the frontier during 1867-1868; Sioux, Cheyenne, Arapahoe, Kiowa,
        Pawnee, Comanche, and Osage depredations in Kansas.

        R-M of J. Lane.   21 Jan.
        HR 8, 41-2, v1, 1p. [1436]
        Depredations by the Arapahoes, Cheyennes, or Sioux in Nebraska during 1865.

        Communication from Capt. Adams.   19 Dec.
        HMD 12, 41-3, v1, 20p. [1462]
        Exploration of the Colorado River area; Indian success at growing crops;
        journal of the expedition; Cocopah, Yuma, Mojave, Chimawava, Paiute, Utah,
        Moquis, Pimo, Maricopa, Apache, Cheyenne, Sioux, and Arapaho Indians dis-
        cussed.

1871   Proceedings of a Council of Indian Tribes.   30 Jan.
        SED 26, 41-3, v1, 23p. [1440]
        Held during Dec. of 1870 at Ocmulgee in the Creek Nation, Indian Territory;
        participating tribes included the Creeks, Seminoles, Cherokees, Choctaws,
        Chickasaws, Osages, Ottawas, Shawnees, Quapaws, Senecas, Sacs, Foxes,
        Wyandotts, and Peorias; not included with the Wichitas, Comanches, Kiowas,
        Cheyennes, and Arapahoes.

        Aid to Civilize the Indians.   23 Jan.
        HED 65, 41-3, v8, 2p. [1454]
        Additional funds needed for the central superintendency: Kickapoos, Ottawas,
        Peorias, Quapaws, Senecas, Wyandotts, Shawnees, Delawares, Wichitas, Kaws,
        Pottawatomies, Kiowas, Comanches, Apaches, Cheyennes, and Arapahoes.

        L-C of J. Bissonnette.   26 Jan.
        HED 80, 41-3, v8, 6p. [1454]
        Sioux, Cheyenne, and Arapaho depredations of 1864-1865 in Dakota.

1871   Depredations by Apache Indians.   11 Feb.
        HED 111, 41-3, v12, 6p. [1460]
        Appropriation to cover the costs of depredations committed in 1870 on freight
        wagons bound for the Cheyenne-Arapaho agency.

        Appropriation for Indian Depredations.   11 Feb.
        HED 123, 41-3, v12, 8p. [1460]
        Apache and Kiowa depredations in 1870 on supplies bound for the Cheyenne-
        Arapaho agency.

        Appropriation for Indian Tribes.   21 Mar.
        HED 11, 42-1, v2, 2p. [1471]
        Subsistence for Arapahoes, Cheyennes, Apaches, Kiowas, and Comanches.

1872   Appropriation for Indian Depredation Claims.   3 Dec.
        HED 11, 42-3, v5, 3p. [1563]
        Against the Cheyennes, Osages, Sioux, Kiowas, Arapahoes, Navajoes, Blackfeet,
        Comanches, and Oregon Indians; list of claims.

        Agreement with the Arapahoes.   19 Dec.
        HED 43, 42-3, v7, 4p. [1565]
        For release of land ceded to them by the treaty of 28 Oct. 1867; negotiations
        to begin with the Cheyennes for relinquishment of their lands.

1873   Mem. of the Kansas Legis.   3 Feb.
        SMD 53, 42-3, v1, 2p. [1546]
        Sioux and Arapaho hostilities; captive taken.

        Resol. of the Kansas Legis.   11 Feb.
        SMD 64, 42-3, v1, 2p. [1546]
        On outrages perpetrated by the Sioux and Arapahoes; captive taken.

        Report on the Territory of Oklahoma.   20 Feb.
        SR 471, 42-3, v3, 2p. [1550]
        Recommends territorial government over Indian Territory; will not affect
        treaties of 1866 with the Choctaws, Chickasaws, Creeks, Cherokees, and
        Seminoles; also, the U.S. has not lost jurisdiction by treaties with the
        Great and Little Osages, Cheyennes, Arapahoes, Pottawatomies, Sacs, Foxes,
        Kiowas, and Comanches.

        Claims Against the Kiowas and Arapahoes.   7 Jan.
        HED 62, 42-3, v7, 16p. [1565]
        For depredations of 1864 in Kansas.

        L-C of H. Wedeles.   9 Jan.
        HED 82, 42-3, v7, 4p. [1565]
        Arapaho depredations of 1867 in Kansas.

        L-C of C. Autobees.   10 Jan.
        HED 89, 42-3, v7, 5p. [1565]
        Comanche, Cheyenne, and Arapaho depredations of 1861-1864 in Colorado.

        L-C of C. Weidner.   25 Feb.
        HED 235, 42-3, v11, 6p. [1569]
        Cheyenne and Arapaho depredations of 1868 in Kansas.

        Agreements with the Cheyennes and Arapahoes.   12 Dec.
        HED 12, 43-1, v8, 5p. [1606]
        Three agreements made 18 Nov. 1873 calling for relinquishment of the reser-
        vation belonging to said tribe under the treaty of 28 Oct. 1867.

        Estimate of Appropriations for Subsistence.   18 Dec.
        HED 23, 43-1, v8, 2p. [1606]
        For Kiowas, Comanches, Cheyennes, Arapahoes, Apaches, and Wichitas in Indian
        Territory.

1874   On the Relief of J. Fletcher.   22 June.
        HR 780, 43-1, v5, 5p. [1627]
        Cheyenne and Arapaho depredations of 1870 in Indian Territory.

1875   Support of Indians in Indian Territory.   13 Jan.
        HED 91, 43-2, v13, 3p. [1646]
        Appropriation to subsist the Cheyenne, Apaches, Arapahoes, Kiowas, Comanches,
        and Wichitas.

1876   Letter on the Cheyennes, Kiowas, Comanches, and Arapahoes.   13 Jan.
        SED 15, 44-1, v1, 2p. [1664]
        Statement of expenditures for support of captive Indians from said tribes.

        Resol. of the Kansas Legis.   6 Mar.
        HMD 121, 44-1, v5, 1p. [1702]
        Opposes reduction of Army strength on the frontier; cites recent hostilities
        of the Sioux, Cheyennes, and Arapahoes.

        R-M of F. Culver.   9 June.
        HR 642, 44-1, v5, 2p. [1712]
        Service in negotiating the treaty of 18 Feb. 1861 with the Cheyennes and
        Arapahoes.

        On the Relief of A. Greenwood.   27 July.
        HR 785, 44-1, v6, 2p. [1713]
        CIA from 1859 to 1861; expenses of expedition to the Arkansas River in 1860
        to make a treaty with the Cheyennes and Arapahoes.

        On the Relief of J. Fletcher.   8 Dec.
        HR 9, 44-2, v1, 3p. [1769]
        Cheyenne and Arapahoe depredations of 1870 between Fort Dodge, Kansas, and
        Camp Supply, Indian Territory.

1877   Increase of the Cavalry Force on the Texas Frontier.   30 Jan.
        HED 33, 44-2, v9, 3p. [1755]
        To control Indian depredations; no Kiowa, Comanche, Cheyenne, or Arapahoe
        raids in the area of Fort Sill; no troops sent to the Sioux war.

1878   On the Relief of J. Fletcher.   14 June.
        SR 521, 45-2, v3, 3p. [1791]
        Cheyenne and Arapahoe depredations of 1870 en route from Fort Dodge, Kansas,
        to Camp Supply, Indian Territory.

        On the Relief of J. Brice.   15 Jan.
        HR 61, 45-2, v1, 2p. [1822]
        Arapahoe depredations of 1868 near Fort Lyon.

        R-C of F. Culver.   15 Feb.
        HR 228, 45-2, v1, 2p. [1822]
        Services in effecting the treaty of 18 Feb. 1861 with the Cheyennes and
        Arapahoes; treaty of 1851 with the Cheyennes, Arapahoes, Kiowas, Comanches,
        and Apaches, and why it failed.

1879   On the Relief of J. Fitzgerald.   21 Jan.
        SR 609, 45-3, v1, 2p. [1837]
        Physician to the Cheyennes and Arapahoes in 1869-1870 near Camp Supply,
        Indian Territory.

        Resol. of Sen. Walker.   16 June.
        SMD 41, 46-1, v1, 1p. [1873]
        Asks information on the following Indian wars: the war in Oregon, Idaho, Cali-
        fornia, and Nevada in 1865-1868; the Cheyenne, Arapaho, Kiowa, and Comanche
        war of 1868-1869 in Kansas, Colorado, and Indian Territory; the Modoc war of
        1872-1873; the Apache war of 1873 in Arizona; the Kiowa, Comanche, and Chey-
        enne war of 1874-1875 in Kansas, Colorado, Texas, Indian Territory, and New

Mexico; the Northern Cheyenne and Sioux war of 1876-1877; the Nez Percé war
of 1877; the Bannock war of 1878; and the Northern Cheyenne war of 1878-1879.

1879   Industrial Training Schools for Indian Youths.   14 June.
HR 29, 46-1, v1, 3p. [1934]
Under treaties with the Cheyennes, Arapahoes, Kiowas, Comanches, Crows,
Navajoes, Sioux, Utes, Northern Cheyennes, and Northern Arapahoes; establish
schools in vacant military posts.

1880   Industrial Training Schools for Indians.   6 Apr.
HR 752, 46-2, v3, 4p. [1936]
Under treaties with, notably, the Cheyennes, Arapahoes, Kiowas, Comanches,
Crows, Navajoes, Sioux, Utes, Northern Cheyennes, and Northern Arapa-
hoes.

R-C of Powers and Newman, and D. and B. Powers.   10 Dec.
HR 7, 46-3, v1, 2p. [1982]
Cheyenne and Arapaho depredations of 1867 between Forts Harker and Wallace.

1881   Deficiency for Indian Supplies.   4 Feb.
SED 34, 46-3, v3, 5p. [1943]
At the Cheyenne and Arapaho, and Kiowa, Comanche, and Wichita agencies in
Indian Territory.

1882   R-P of Powers and Newman, and D. and B. Powers.   4 Apr.
SR 375, 47-1, v3, 2p. [2006]
Cheyenne and Arapaho depredations of 1867 between Forts Harker and Wallace.

Fort McKinney, Wyoming.   6 Apr.
HED 160, 47-1, v22, 10p. [2030]
Appropriation for construction; located in buffalo region resorted to by the
Sioux, Northern Cheyennes, and Arapahoes.

Confirmation of Land in Indian Territory.   12 Apr.
HED 169, 47-1, v22, 4p. [2030]
To the Cheyennes and Arapahoes; set apart by an Executive Order of 10 Aug.
1869 in lieu of land set apart by the treaty of 28 Oct. 1867.

Personal Assaults in Indian Territory.   22 Apr.
HED 181, 47-1, v22, 4p. [2030]
Cheyenne Indian attempts to kill the U.S. agent at the Cheyenne and Arapaho
Agency; jurisdictional concerns.

R-P of Powers and Newman, and D. and B. Powers.   14 Feb.
SR 407, 47-1, v2, 2p. [2066]
Cheyenne and Arapaho depredations of 1867 between Forts Harker and Wallace.

R-P of J. Fletcher.   14 Feb.
HR 408, 47-1, v2, 2p. [2066]
Cheyenne and Arapaho depredations of 1870 in Indian Territory.

1883   Land in Indian Territory.   19 Dec.
SED 13, 48-1, v1, 82p. [2162]
Confirmation of land title to the Cheyennes and Arapahoes, and the Wichitas,
Caddoes, and affiliated bands.

1884   On the Case of J. Foster.   15 Feb.
SED 105, 48-1, v6, 15p. [2167]
Jurisdictional matters involving the case of the murder of an Arapaho by a
Creek Indian in Indian Territory.

R-P of J. Fletcher.   24 Apr.
HR 1344, 48-1, v5, 3p. [2257]
Cheyenne and Arapaho depredations of 1870 in Indian Territory.

1885   Cheyenne and Arapaho Indians. 5 Jan.
        SED 16, 48-2, v1 (pt. 1), 27p. [2261]
        On the condition of said Indians in Indian Territory; disarming the Indians
        to promote civilization.

1886   R-C of J. Fletcher. 13 Apr.
        SR 502, 49-1, v5, 3p. [2359] or HR 3624, 49-1, v1, 3p. [2500]
        Cheyenne and Arapaho depredations; 1870.

        Monographs of the U.S. Geological Survey. (no date)
        HMD 397, 49-1, v27, 770p. [2433]
        Volume 12; mining in Colorado; area often warred over by the Arapahoes and
        Utes.

        R-P of J. Brice. 1 May.
        HR 2173, 49-1, v7, 1p. [2441]
        Arapaho depredations of 1868 in Missouri.

        R-C of G. Maxwell et al. 17 June.
        HR 2885, 49-1, v10, 3p. [2444]
        Cheyenne, Arapaho, Kiowa, and Comanche depredations of 1865-1870 in Kansas,
        and Indian Territory.

1887   R-C of J. Hobbs. 28 Feb.
        SR 1970, 49-2, v3, 1p. [2458] or HR 2713, 49-1, v9, 2p. [2443]
        Supplies furnished during negotiations with Cheyennes and Arapahoes; 1860.

        R-C of A. Culver. 28 Feb.
        SR 1972, 49-2, v3, 3p. [2458]
        Supplies furnished during negotiations with Cheyennes and Arapahoes; 1860.

1888   R-C of H. Wedeles. 29 Mar.
        HR 1482, 50-1, v5, 4p. [2602]
        Arapaho depredations of 1867 in Kansas.

        R-C of H. Newman. 17 Apr.
        HR 1787, 50-1, v6, 3p. [2603]
        Kiowa, Cheyenne, Arapaho, and Comanche depredations.

        R-C of I. Fieldhouse. 14 July.
        HR 2876, 50-1, v8, 2p. [2605]
        Sioux, Northern Cheyenne, and Northern Arapaho depredations of 1874 in
        Wyoming.

1889   Subsistence and Civilization Funds. 16 Dec.
        HED 52, 51-1, v26, 2p. [2741]
        Diversion of funds from the Arapahoes, Cheyennes, Kiowas, Comanches, Wichi-
        tas, and affiliated bands, to the Northern Cheyennes in Montana.

1890   On the Case of J. Sechler. 13 Jan.
        SR 76, 51-1, v1, 1p. [2703] or HR 584, 51-1, v2, 1p. [2808]
        Land title in Colorado; Cheyenne and Arapaho treaty of 14 Oct. 1865.

        L-C of Jones, Russell, and Co. 20 Feb.
        HED 220, 51-1, v32, 2p. [2747]
        Cheyenne and Arapaho depredations.

        L-C of T. Owen. 26 Sept.
        HED 469, 51-1, v37, 3p. [2752]
        Arapaho depredations of 1872 in New Mexico.

        Cession of Certain Indian Lands. 4 Dec.
        SED 1, 51-2, v1, 24p. [2818]
        Agreement of 1890 with the Cheyenne and Arapaho Indians for cession of their
        lands in Indian Territory; belong to them under the treaty of 28 Oct. 1867;
        allotments to be made.

1891   Additional Subsistence for Indians.   5 Jan.
       HED 139, 51-2, v33, 3p. [2863]
       Appropriation for principally the Yankton Sioux, Arickarees, Mandans, Gros
       Ventres, Northern Arapahoes, Sisseton Sioux, and Devil's Lake Sioux.

       Agreement with Cheyennes and Arapahoes.   13 Jan.
       HR 3441, 51-2, v1, 5p. [2885]
       Made in Oct. of 1890; calls for allotment, and cession of lands in that part
       of Indian Territory known as the "Cherokee outlet"; treaty of 28 Oct. 1867.

1892   An Act to Pay Choctaws and Chickasaws.   18 Feb.
       SED 42, 52-1, v5, 41p. [2900]
       For lands in Oklahoma Territory now occupied by Cheyennes and Arapahoes.

       Mem. of the Chickasaw Indians.   26 Feb.
       SMD 82, 52-1, v2, 13p. [2904]
       On whether lands ceded by the treaty of 28 Apr. 1866 were ceded "in trust,"
       or were ceded "absolutely" to the U.S.; lands occupied by the Cheyenne and
       Arapaho Indians only temporarily to be opened for settlement.

       Mem. of the Choctaw Nation.   14 Mar.
       SMD 95, 52-1, v2, 25p. [2904]
       Agreement between the U.S. and the Cheyennes and Arapahoes to open land up
       for settlement; Choctaws insist that these lands belong to them, as they
       were merely held in trust by the U.S.

       Resol. of Sen. Jones.   13 Apr.
       SMD 126, 52-1, v5, 1p. [2907]
       Payments to the Choctaw and Chickasaw Nations for their interest in the
       Cheyenne and Arapaho reservation of Indian Territory.

       Choctaw and Chickasaw Indians.   13 Apr.
       SR 552, 52-1, v3, 35p. [2913] or HR 1661, 52-1, v7, 35p. [3048]
       On the proposed act to pay said Indians for lands now occupied by the Chey-
       enne and Arapaho Indians; land title at issue, with various treaty stipu-
       lations involved; lands are being ceded to the government, and will be part
       of Oklahoma.

       Cheyenne and Arapaho Lands.   5 Jan.
       HED 10, 52-1, v29, 1p. [2949]
       Appropriation for allotments to be made in Oklahoma Territory; agreement of
       Oct., 1890, calling for land cessions.

       Shoshone and Arapaho Indians.   11 Jan.
       HED 70, 52-1, v33, 61p. [2953]
       Cession and relinquishment of part of the Wind River reservation in Wyoming;
       agreement of 2 Oct. 1891.

       Support of the Cheyennes and Arapahoes.   16 Apr.
       HED 198, 52-1, v35, 4p. [2955]
       Appropriation for fiscal 1893; Oklahoma Territory.

       Resol. of Rep. Peel.   17 June.
       HMD 275, 52-1, v1, 1p. [2959]
       On payments to the Choctaw and Chickasaw Nations for their interest in the
       Cheyenne and Arapaho reservation.

       Opening Lands to Settlement.   27 Feb.
       HR 478, 52-1, v2, 1p. [3043]
       Acquired under an agreement with the Cheyenne and Arapaho Indians.

       Additional Justices for the Supreme Court of Oklahoma.   17 May.
       HR 1413, 52-1, v5, 3p. [3046]
       Seven new counties to be formed out of the Cheyenne and Arapaho reservation;
       increased population and case load.

1893   Rights to Settlers in Oklahoma.   4 Oct.
        HR 73, 53-1, v1, 3p. [3157]
        Located on Absentee Shawnee, Pottawatomie, Cheyenne, Arapaho, Iowa, Sac, and
        Fox lands in Oklahoma Territory.

        Deficiency Estimates for the Interior Dept.   13 Dec.
        HED 37, 53-2, v26, 3p. [3223]
        Cost of advertising Cheyenne and Arapaho lands open for settlement.

1894   R-C of J. Morrison.   26 Apr.
        SR 367, 53-2, v5, 3p. [3183] or HR 564, 53-2, v2, 3p. [3270]
        Land title issue in Oklahoma; Arapaho and Cheyenne agreement of 1890, calling
        for allotments, and land cessions.

        Negotiations with Shoshones and Arapahoes.   3 Jan.
        HED 51, 53-2, v26, 19p. [3223]
        Agreement of 2 Oct. 1891 for land cessions in Wyoming not ratified; negotia-
        tions reopened, but no new agreement is made; council proceedings.

        Settlers on Public Lands in Oklahoma.   17 Jan.
        HR 263, 53-2, v1, 3p. [3269]
        Lands ceded by the Sacs, Foxes, Iowas, Citizen band of Pottawatomies, Absen-
        tee Shawnees, Cheyennes, and Arapahoes.

        Kansas City, Oklahoma, and Pacific Railway Co.   12 July.
        HR 1232, 53-2, v4, 2p. [3272]
        Right of way through Cheyenne and Arapaho lands in Oklahoma and Indian
        Territory.

        R-P of Sharp Nose.   1 Aug.
        HR 1352, 53-2, v4, 3p. [3272]
        War chief of the Northern Arapahoes serves U.S. as an Indian scout.

        Town-site Entries in Oklahoma.   7 Aug.
        HR 1379, 53-2, v4, 5p. [3272]
        Legal issues surrounding entries; Sac, Fox, Iowa, Pottawatomie, Shawnee,
        Cheyenne, Arapaho, and Cherokee land cessions.

1895   Lands in Oklahoma.   21 Jan.
        SR 795, 53-3, v1, 12p. [3288]
        Claims of newspapers for the expenses of advertising the opening of Cheyenne
        and Arapaho lands.

1896   Agreement with the Shoshones and Arapahoes.   8 May.
        SD 247, 54-1, v8, 17p. [3354]
        Made 21 Apr. 1896; land cessions in Wyoming; council proceedings.

        Construction of a Government Road.   27 Apr.
        SR 798, 54-1, v4, 3p. [3365]
        Between Fort Washakie on the Shoshone reservation, and Yellowstone Park;
        through Shoshone, Bannock, and Arapaho hunting grounds.

        Northern Cheyenne and Arapaho Indians.   18 Feb.
        HD 249, 54-1, v58, 4p. [3425]
        Use of unexpended appropriations to purchase cattle for the Tongue River
        reservation, Montana.

        Rights of Indians to Hunt on Unoccupied Public Domain.   31 Jan.
        HR 206, 54-1, v1, 3p. [3457]
        Bill calling for the surrender or modification of Shoshone, Bannock, and
        Arapaho hunting privileges in Wyoming and Idaho.

        Title to Certain Lands.   20 Apr.
        HR 1375, 54-1, v5, 3p. [3461]
        Bill to quit title to land; includes lands ceded by Cherokees, Cheyennes,
        Arapahoes, Absentee Shawnees, and Pottawatomies.

1896   Settlers in Oklahoma.   1 May.
        HR 1581, 54-1, v6, 2p. [3462]
        Bill affecting settlers whose entries on Cheyenne, Arapaho, or Cherokee
        lands were less than 160 acres.

        Military Road in Wyoming.   7 May.
        HR 1659, 54-1, v7, 2p. [3463]
        Would traverse the hunting grounds of Indians from the Shoshone reservation.

B

CIS U.S. Serial Set Index

The following entries pertaining to the Arapaho Indians have been derived from the multivolume CIS U.S. Serial Set Index (Washington, DC: Congressional Information Service, © 1975-1979). The Index covers the complete set of publications issued in the Congressional Serial Set and American State Papers from 1789 to 1969. Permission to reprint the material below, copyrighted by Congressional Information Service, Inc., 4520 East-West Highway, Bethesda, MD 20814-3389, is hereby gratefully acknowledged.

Each entry consists of a descriptive title and document citation, which includes reference to publication series (e.g., S. exdoc.), publication number e.g., 35), number of the Congress and session (e.g., 36-1), and serial volume number (e.g., 1031). Thus, "S.exdoc. 35 (36-1) 1031" is to be read in full as "Senate Executive Document number 35, 36th Congress, 1st session, Serial Set volume number 1031."

With a few exceptions, the order of the entries according to the Serial Set number coincides with the chronological order. The entries are reprinted exactly as they appear in CIS U.S. Serial Set Index.

The following abbreviations are used:

doc.	Document
exdoc.	Executive document
H.	House
misdoc.	Miscellaneous document
rp.	report
S.	Senate

Estimate of amounts required to hold councils with Kiowas, Comanches, and other Indians who roam near Arkansas river, west of 100th degree west longitude; Arrapahoes and Cheyennes, located below south fork of Platte river; Sioux and other Indians of the plains, and Red Lake Chippewas and Indians of Red river, in Minnesota, for extinguishment of their title to lands in Minnesota
S.exdoc. 35 (36-1) 1031

Estimate of appropriations for survey of land for benefit of Cheyenne and Arapahoe Indians
H.exdoc. 104 (40-2)1337

Estimate of appropriations required for fulfilling treaty stipulations with Northern Cheyenne and Arapaho Indians, under treaty of May 10,1868
S.exdoc. 23 (40-3) 1360

Letter from Commissioner of Indian Affairs asking appropriation of $250,000 for purchase of subsistence for Arapaho, Cheyenne, and other tribes for 1871
H.exdoc. 261 (41-2) 1426

Appropriation for purchase of supplies for Arapaho, Cheyenne, Apache, Kiowa, and Comanche Indians
H.exdoc. 11 (42-1) 1471

Outrages perpetrated by Sioux and Arapaho Indians. Resolutions of legislature of Kansas
S.misdoc. 64 (42-3) 1546

Release of lands ceded to Cheyenne and Arapaho Indians
H.exdoc. 43 (42-3) 1565

Claims for depredations by Kiowa and Arapaho Indians, 1864
H.exdoc. 62 (42-3) 1565

Agreements with Cheyenne and Arapaho Indians
H.exdoc. 12 (43-1) 1606

Support of Cheyenne, Arapahoe, Apache, Kiowa, Comanche, and Wichita Indians
H.exdoc. 91 (43-2) 1646

Captive Cheyenne, Arapahoe, Kiowa, and Comanche Indians
S.exdoc. 15 (44-1) 1664

Letters from agents of Cheyenne and Arapahoe, and Kiowa, Comanche, and Wichita agencies, Indian Territory, on deficiency estimate
S.exdoc. 34 (46-3) 1943

Message of President on confirmation of certain lands in Indian Territory to Arapahoe and Cheyenne Indians
H.exdoc. 169 (47-1) 2030

Papers on jurisdiction of U.S. in case of Johnson Foster, Creek Indian accused of killing Arapahoe
S.exdoc. 105 (48-1) 2167

Resolution requesting papers in case of Johnson Foster, Creek Indian accused of killing Arapahoe
S.misdoc. 43 (48-1) 2171

Message of President on condition of Cheyenne and Arapaho Indians
S.exdoc. 16 (48-2) 2261

Claims for depredations committed by Cheyenne, Arapahoe, Kiowa, and Comanche tribes of Indians
H.rp. 2885 (49-1) 2444

Message of President transmitting agreement by Cherokee Commission with Cheyenne and Arapahoe Indians for cession of certain lands
S.exdoc. 1 (51-2) 2818

Confirming agreement with Cheyenne and Arapahoe Indians
H.rp. 3441 (51-2) 2885

Resolution on Cheyenne and Arapaho Reservation
S.misdoc. 126 (52-1) 2907

Lands of Cheyennes and Arapahoes in Oklahoma Territory
H.exdoc. 10 (52-1) 2949

Message of President transmitting agreement with Shoshone and Arapaho Indians
H.exdoc. 70 (52-1) 2953

Estimate of appropriation for support Cheyenne and Arapaho Indians
H.exdoc. 198 (52-1) 2955

Opening to settlement lands acquired from Cheyenne and Arapaho Indians
H.rp. 478 (52-1) 3043

Letters of Commissioner of Indian Affairs on certain negotiations with Shoshone and Arapahoe Indians for surrender of portions of reservation in Wyoming
H.exdoc. 51 (53-2) 3223

Agreement with Shoshone and Arapaho Indians of Wind River Reservation
S.doc. 247 (54-1) 3354

Cattle for Northern Cheyenne and Arapaho Indians
H.doc. 249 (54-1) 3425

Negotiation of hunting rights with Shoshone, Arapahoe, and Bannock Indians in
Wyoming and Idaho
H.rp. 206 (54-1) 3457

Sale of lands of Cheyenne and Arapaho Agency and Arapaho School
S.rp. 184 (60-1) 5218

Appropriation for subsistence and civilization of Northern Cheyennes and Arapahos
S.rp. 563 (60-1) 5219

Sale of certain lands of Cheyenne and Arapaho Indians and Arapaho School in Oklahoma
H.rp. 1640 (60-1) 5226

Sale of 640 acres of Cheyenne and Arapaho Agency and Arapaho School
S.doc. 64 (60-1) 5267

Settlement and entry of Cheyenne and Arapaho lands in Oklahoma
S.rp. 552 (61-2) 5583; H.rp. 574 (61-2) 5591

Sale of land in Cheyenne and Arapaho Reservation to Masons in Oklahoma
H.rp.2033 (61-3) 5848

Time for payment for lands in Cheyenne and Arapaho Reservation, Okla.
S.rp. 908 (64-2) 7106

Time for payment for lands in Cheyenne and Arapaho Reservation, Oklahoma
H.rp. 1324 (64-2) 7110

To refer claims of Arapaho and Cheyenne Indians to Court of Claims
S.rp. 534 (66-2) 7649

Cheyenne and Arapahoe Indians to file suit in Ct. of Cls.
S.rp. 971 (69-1) 8526; H.rp. 1361 (69-1) 8534

Claims of Arapaho and Cheyenne Indians
S.rp. 496 (70-1) 8829; H.rp. 954 (70-1) 8836

Per capita payment to Shoshoni and Arapaho Indians
S.rp. 789 (70-1) 8830; H.rp. 1238 (70-1) 8837

Per capita payments to Shoshoni and Arapaho Indians
S.rp. 261 (71-2) 9185; H.rp. 886 (71-2) 9191; S.rp. 1244 (71-3) 9323;
H.rp. 2274 (71-3) 9326

Arapahoe and Cheyenne Indians to submit claims to Court of Claims
S.rp. 465 (74-1) 9878; H.rp. 1091 (74-1) 9888; S.rp. 291 (75-1) 10076;
H.rp. 1293 (75-1) 10085; S.rp. 100 (76-1) 10292; S.rp. 460 (77-1) 10545;
H.rp. 764 (77-1) 10555; S.rp. 86 (78-1) 10755

Eliminating part of Seger School reserve and setting it aside for Cheyenne and
Arapahoe Indians of Oklahoma
S.rp. 986 (75-1) 10077

Eliminating part of Seger School reserve and setting it aside for Cheyenne and
Arapaho Indians of Oklahoma
H.rp. 1991 (75-3) 10234

Setting aside lands in Oklahoma for Cheyenne-Arapaho Tribes of Indians, etc.
S.rp. 856 (77-1) 10546

Setting aside lands in Oklahoma for Cheyenne-Arapaho Tribes of Indians
H.rp. 896 (77-1) 10555

Expenditure of trust funds held in joint ownership by Shoshone and Arapaho tribes
ot Wind River Reservation
S.rp. 117 (80-1) 11114; H.rp. 172 (80-1) 11118

Setting aside lands in Fort Reno military reservation in trust for Cheyenne Arapaho
Tribes of Oklahoma
H.rp. 1323 (81-1) 11301

Setting aside lands in Fort Reno Military Reservation for Cheyenne-Arapaho Tribes
of Indians. 2 pts.
S.rp. 2246 (81-2) 11371

American Ethnology Bur. bull. 148; Arapaho child life and its cultural background
H.doc. 626 (81-2) 11478

Per capita payments to Shoshone and Arapaho Indians
S.rp. 541 (82-1) 11488; H.rp. 863 (82-1) 11498

Setting aside lands in Fort Reno military reservation for Cheyenne-Arapaho Tribes
of Oklahoma
H.rp. 1935 (82-2) 11577

Increase payments from trust funds to Shoshone and Arapaho tribes
S.rp. 263 (83-1) 11659

Compensation to Shoshone and Arapaho Indians for lands of Riverton project
S.rp. 644 (83-1) 11661

Amending act of May 19, 1947, so as to increase payments from trust funds to
Shoshone and Arapaho Tribes
H.rp. 261 (83-1) 11664

Compensation to Shoshone and Arapahoe Indians for lands ceded to Riverton project
H.rp. 269 (83-1) 11664

Per capita payments to members of Shoshone and Arapahoe Indian Tribes to be made
quarterly
S.rp. 1168 (84-1) 11817; H.rp. 1486 (84-1) 11824

Authorizing conveyance of land from Shoshone and Arapahoe Indian Tribes of Wind
River Reservation in Wyoming to U.S.
S.rp. 2231 (84-2) 11889

Amending act of May 19, 1947, to extend time for making payments to members of
Shoshone and Arapahoe Tribes
S.rp. 2369 (84-2) 11889

Amend act of May 19, 1947, to extend time for making payments to Shoshone and
Arapaho Indians of Wyoming
H.rp. 2592 (84-2) 11900

Authorizing conveyance of tribal lands from Shoshone and Arapaho Indians of
Wind River Reservation to U.S.
H.rp. 2706 (84-2) 11900

Conference report on conveyance of tribal lands from Shoshone Indian Tribe and
Arapahoe Indian Tribe
H.rp. 2956 (84-2) 11901

Amending act of May 19, 1947 relative to trust funds of Shoshone and Arapahoe
Tribes
S.rp. 1869 (85-2) 12063

Conveying certain lands in Oklahoma for Cheyenne and Arapaho Indians
S.rp. 2335 (85-2) 12065

Setting aside certain lands in Oklahoma for Cheyenne and Arapaho Indians
H.rp. 1666 (85-2) 12073

Amending act relating of trust funds of Shoshone and Arapahoe Tribes
H.rp. 1842 (85-2) 12073

Setting aside certain lands in Oklahoma for Cheyenne and Arapaho Indians
H.rp. 378 (86-1) 12160; S.rp. 1617 (86-2) 12236

Land for Cheyenne and Arapaho Tribes
S.rp. 456 (90-1) 12750-2

Funds of Cheyenne-Arapaho Tribes
S.rp. 530 (90-1) 12750-3

Judgment funds of Cheyenne-Arapaho Tribes
H.rp. 624 (90-1) 12753-4

Convey lands to Cheyenne and Arapaho Tribes, Okla.
H.rp. 1325 (90-2) 12795-2

C

CIS U.S. Congressional Committee Hearings Index

The following entries pertaining to the Arapaho Indians have been derived from the multivolume CIS U.S. Congressional Committee Hearings Index (Washington, DC: Congressional Information Service, © 1981-1985) and the annual supplements thereto. Permission to reprint the material below, copyrighted by Congressional Information Service, Inc., 4520 East-West Highway, Bethesda, MD 20814-3389, is hereby gratefully acknowledged.

Each entry consists of a brief description of the contents of the document, an accession number (e.g., H195-5), date(s) of the hearing(s) (e.g., Mar. 23, 1918), number of the Congress and session (e.g., 65-2), collation data (e.g., 169-193 p.), and the bill number, if applicable, with the Congress in parentheses [e.g., (65) H.R. 2614]. Thus, "H195-5. Mar. 23, 1918. 65-2. 169-193 p. (65) H.R. 2614" is to be read in full as "House of Representatives accession number 195-5 of hearings held on March 23, 1918, 65th Congress, 2d session, pages 169-193, House of Representatives (65th Congress) bill number 2614."

The entries, which are arranged chronologically, are reproduced as they appear in the Index.

Peyote use by Indians, prohibition.
H195-5. Mar. 23, 1918. 65-2. 169-193 p. (65) H.R. 2614.

Land allotments and per capita payment, authorization.
H497-2. Mar. 1, 1928. 70-1. ii + 4 p. (70) H.R. 11365.

Claims deadline extension.
H497-4. Mar. 1, 15, 1928. 70-1. ii + 12 p. (70) H.R. 11359.

Okla Indians conditions survey.
S545-5-A. Nov. 17-22, 1930. 71-2. vi + 6645-7472 + xv p. Index.

Wyo, Idaho, and Utah Indians conditions survey.
S451-5-A. Sept. 12-14, 1932. 72-1. iv + 14427-14806 + xi p. Index.

Mont Indians conditions survey.
S471-0-B. Oct. 17-19, 21, Nov. 9, 1933. 73-1. iv + 16511-16946 + ix p. Index.

Indians self govt, land allotment, and land dev programs authorization.
H680-5-C; S474-3. May 2, 1934. 73-2. ii + 261-314 p. (73) H.R. 7902.
Apr. 26, 28, 30, May 3, 4, 17, 1934. 73-2. iv + 57-429 p. (73) S. 2755; (73) S. 3645.

Okla Indians gen welfare program review.
(74) S489-4. Apr. 8-11, 1935. 74-1. iv + 153 p. (74) S. 2047.

Indian tribes in Calif, conditions review.
(76) S637-0. On various dates between Apr. 6, 1936, and Apr. 29, 1940. 74-2; 75-1; 75-3; 76-1; 76-3. iv + 20447-22022 + v p. Index. (75) H.R. 5472; (74) H.R. 7902; (74) H.R. 7781; (76) S. 415; (76) S. 626; (76) S.2103; (76) S. 2137; (76) S. 2318; (76) S. 2334; (75) S. 858; (75) S. 1736; (75) H.R. 7230; (75) S. 3745; (75) S. 3903; (76) S. 2089.

Court of Claims, jurisdiction estab.
(76) H864-10. June 20, 1939. 76-1. iii + 37 p. (76) H.R. 2775.

Indian aff admin investigation.
(78) H1051-0. July 23, 25, 27, 29, 31, Aug. 2, 4-6, 8, Oct. 1, 3, Nov. 11, 14, 15, 21, 22, Dec. 5, 1944. 78-2. xiv + 1168 p.

Shoshone and Arapaho Indians trust funds distribution to tribes.
(80) H1140-3. Mar. 15, 1947. 80-1. iii + 40 p. (80) H.R. 1098.

Fort Reno Military Reservation, Okla, land conveyance to Cheyenne and Arapaho Indians.
(81) H1264-3; (82) H1380-3. June 27-30, July 21, Aug. 10, 17, 1949. 81-1. iii + 180 p. (81) H.R. 4756. Mar. 4, 5, Apr. 5, 1952. 82-2. iii + 48 p. (82) H.R. 1631.

Arapahoe Business Council, oil and gas produced on Fed lands, Geological Survey royalty programs.
H441-14.6. Sept. 23, Oct. 6, 1981. 97-1. vii + 848 p. il.

Arapaho Business Council, Indian health programs, FY 85-FY 88; authorization.
S961-15.2. Mar. 17, 1984. 98-2. vi + 467 p.

Arapaho Business Council, Indian tribes land consolidation and inheritance law, tribal authority clarifications and technical corrections.
3 S411-5.2. July 31, 1984. 98-2. iv + 81 p.

D

United States government publications

The following entries pertaining to the Arapaho Indians have been derived from the periodical listings of United States government publications, issued since 1885 under various titles, among them United States' Publications: Monthly Catalogue; United States Government Publications: A Monthly Catalogue; Catalogue of Publications Issued by the Government of the United States; Catalogue of United States Public Documents; Monthly Catalogue [of] United States Public Documents; and Monthly Catalog of United States Government Publications.

The entries, arranged below according to the month and year of publication and the page of the catalog in which they are listed, are reprinted exactly as they appear in the original source, including inconsistencies in spelling and capitalization.

The following abbreviations are used:

Cong.	Congress
Ex. Doc.	Executive document
h., H. R.	House of Representatives
no.	number
p(p).	page(s)
rep., rp.	report
S., Sen.	Senate
sess.	session

January 1890, p. 11
Letter from the Commissioner of Indian Affairs. On the application of funds appropriated for the subsistence and civilization of Arapahoes, Cheyennes, Apaches, Kiowas, Comanches, Wichitas, etc., to the purchase of subsistence for Northern Cheyenne Indians at Tongue river agency, Montana. December 16, 1889. 2 pp. H. R. Ex. Doc., no. 52; 51st Cong., 1st sess.

June 1891, p. 167
Agreement by the Cherokee commission with the Cheyenne and Arapahoe indians for the cession of lands; December 4, 1890; 24 pp. Sen. ex. doc. no. 1; 51st Cong., 2d sess.

June 1891, p. 168
Report from the committee on indian affairs. To ratify an agreement with the Cheyenne and Arapaho indians in Oklahoma; January 13, 1891; 5 pp. H. R. rep. no. 3441; 51st Cong., 2d sess.

October 1892, p. 239
Letters from the Secretary of the Interior in relation to the allotment of lands to the Cheyenne and Arapahoes in Oklahoma. January 5, 1892. 1 p. H. R. ex. doc. no. 13; 52d Cong., 1st sess.

October 1892, p. 240
Agreement between the Shoshone and Arapahoe Indians of the Shoshone and Wind river reservation and the commission appointed under the act of March 3, 1891. January 11, 1892. 61 pp. H. R. ex. doc. no. 70; 52d Cong., 1st sess.

October 1892, p. 241
Message from the President relative to the act to pay the Choctaw and Chickasaw Indians for certain lands now occupied by the Cheyenne and Arapahoe Indians. February 18, 1892. 41 pp. Sen. ex. doc. no. 42; 52d Cong., 1st sess.

December 1892, p. 303
Report made to 52d Congress, 1st session: To open to settlement lands acquired from
the Cheyenne and Arapahoe indians; February 27, 1892; 1 p. (h. 478.)

December 1892, p. 304
Report made to 52d Congress, 1st session: Relating to claim of the Choctaw and
Chickasaw indians for lands occupied by the Cheyenne and Arapahoe indians;
June 17, 1892; 35 pp. (h. 1661.)

April 1893, p. 89
Letter from the Secretary of the Interior. Relative to the act to pay Choctaw and
Chickasaw Indians for certain lands now occupied by the Cheyenne and Arapahoe In-
dians; April 13, 1893; 35 pp., 18 maps. Sen. ex. doc. no. 552; 52d Cong., 1st. sess.

August 1903, p. 335
President of United States: Opening additional lands, Cheyenne and Arapahoe Reservation, proclamation. [Aug. 12, 1903.] 1 p.

June 1904, p. 427
Congress of United States, Laws: Statutes passed at 1st and 2d sessions of 58th
Congress, 1903-04, and concurrent resolutions, recent treaties and executive
proclamations; edited under direction of Secretary of State. 1904 [414] p. ....
Cheyenne and Arapahoe Reservation, Proclamation opening additional lands. ....

December 1909, p. 241
House, Indian Affairs Committee: McGuire, B. S. Report favoring H. 14579, to amend
act to authorize Secretary of Interior to issue patents in fee to purchasers of
Indian lands under any law now existing or hereafter enacted [so as to permit Grand
Lodge, A. F. A. M., of Oklahoma to purchase land and buildings thereon, of school
and agency reservation tract within Cheyenne and Arapaho Reservation]. Dec. 20,
1909. 2 p. (H. rp. 45.)

January 1910, p. 325
Senate, Indian Affairs Committee: Clapp, M. E. Report amending H. 14579, to amend
act to authorize Secretary of Interior to issue patents in fee to purchasers of
Indian lands under any law now existing or hereafter enacted [so as to permit Grand
Lodge, A. F. A. M., of Oklahoma to purchase land and buildings thereon, of school
and agency reservation tract within Cheyenne and Arapaho Reservation]. Jan. 20,
1910. 2 p. (S. rp. 108.)

February 1910, p. 399
Public laws [61st Congress, 2d session] public [act] 24-62; approved Jan. 28
[-Feb. 25, 1910]: Grand Lodge, A. F. A. M., of Oklahoma. H. 14579, to amend act to
authorize Secretary of Interior to issue patents in fee to purchasers of Indian
lands under any law now existing or hereafter enacted [so as to permit lodge to
purchase land and buildings thereon, of school and agency reservation tract within
Cheyenne and Arapahoe Reservation]. Jan. 31. 1 p. (No. 29.)

March 1910, p. 497
House, Indian Affairs Committee: McGuire, B. S. Report amending H. 8914, to open
to settlement and entry under general provisions of homestead laws certain lands in
Oklahoma [heretofore reserved for Cheyenne and Arapahoe school and agency purposes].
Feb. 26, 1910. 2 p. (H. rp. 574.)

April 1910, p. 616
Senate, Indian Affairs Committee: Clapp, M. E. Report favoring H. 8914, to open to
settlement and entry under general provisions of homestead laws certain lands in
Oklahoma [heretofore reserved for Cheyenne and Arapahoe school and agency purposes].
Apr. 14, 1910. 2 p. (S. rp. 552.)

June 1910, p. 770
Public laws [61st Congress, 2d session] public [act] 194-323; approved [May 30-]
June 25, 1910: Cheyenne and Arapaho Reservation, H. 8914, to open to settlement and
entry under general provisions of homestead laws certain lands in Oklahoma [hereto-
fore reserved for Cheyenne and Arapaho school and agency purposes].   [June 17.] 2 p.
(No. 215.)

July 1910, p. 39
President of United States: Cheyenne and Arapaho Reservation, Okla. Opening lands in
Cheyenne and Arapahoe Reservation, proclamation.   July 1, 1910. 1 p. (No. 1057.)

February 1911, p. 410
[61st Congress, 3d session] public [act] 337-403; approved Feb. 2-20, 1911: Grand
Lodge, A. F. A. M., of Oklahoma. H. 29300, to sell 40-acre tract of land [in Cheyenne and Arapaho Reservation] to masonic order in Oklahoma.   Feb. 20. 1 p. (No. 400.)

February 1911, p. 415
House, Indian Affairs Committee: Campbell, P. P. Report amending H. 18893, relating
to title of lands inherited by minor heirs of Indian allottees [of Cheyenne and
Arapaho and Kiowa reservations, Okla.], and sold by order of court. Feb. 2, 1911.
3 p. (H. rp. 2047.)

February 1911, p. 449
Senate, Public Lands Committee: Thornton, J. R.   Report favoring H. 29300, to sell
40-acre tract of land [in Cheyenne and Arapaho Reservation] to masonic order in
Oklahoma.   Feb. 9, 1911. 3 p. (S. rp. 1113.)

February 1911, p. 460
Justice Department: Griffin, George M.   In Court of Claims, Indian depredations,
Griffin v. United States and Cheyenne and Arapaho tribes of Indians, no. 9591; Ira
W. Olive, surviving partner of firm of Isom P. and Ira W. Olive v. [same], no. 9910;
defendants' brief. [1911.] p. 17-45.

February 1911, p. 461
Justice Department: Olive, Isom P.   In Court of Claims, Indian depredations, Andrew
J. Anthony, admr. of Olive, v. United States and Cheyenne and Arapahoe Indians,
no. 9909; defendants' brief. [1911.] p. 111-142.

June 1911, p. 689
Senate, Indian Affairs Committee: Gamble, R. J.   Report amending S. 2355, extending
time for payment of balance due on purchase price of tract of land [in Cheyenne and
Arapaho Reservation, purchased by Grand Lodge, A. F. A. M., of Oklahoma].   June 12,
1911. 2 p. (S. rp. 62.)

August 1911, p. 85
Public laws [62d Congress, 1st session] public [act] 5-45; approved [August 8-]22,
1911: Cheyenne and Arapaho Reservation. H. 12534, to extend time of payment of
balance due for lands sold under act [to open to settlement and entry under general
provisions of homestead laws certain lands in Oklahoma heretofore reserved for Cheyenne and Arapaho school and agency purposes].   Aug. 22. 1 p. (No. 43.)

August 1911, p. 90
House, Indian Affairs Committee: Stephens, J. H.   Report amending H. 12534, to extend time of payment of balance due under act [to open to settlement and
entry under general provisions of homestead laws certain lands in Oklahoma heretofore reserved for Cheyenne and Arapaho school and agency purposes].   Aug. 8, 1911.
2 p. (H. rp. 136.)

August 1911, p. 98
Senate, Indian Affairs Committee: Owen, R. L.   Report amending S. 3151, to extend
time of payment of balance due for lands sold under act [to open to settlement and
entry under general provisions of homestead laws certain lands in Oklahoma heretofore
reserved for Cheyenne and Arapaho school and agency purposes].   Aug. 4, 1911. 2 p.
(S. rp. 126.)

December 1911, p. 306
Public laws [62d Congress, 2d session] public [act] 46-53; approved Dec. 8[-Dec. 22, 1911]: Grand Lodge, A. F. A. M., of Oklahoma. S. 2355, extending time for payment of balance due on purchase price of tract of land [in Cheyenne and Arapaho Reservation, purchased by lodge]. Dec. 21. 1 p. (No. 48.)

December 1911, p. 309
House, Indian Affairs Committee: Carter, C. D. Report amending H. 2853, extending time for payment of balance due on purchase price of tract of land [in Cheyenne and Arapaho Reservation, purchased by Grand Lodge, A. F. A. M., of Oklahoma]. Dec. 8, 1911. 2 p. (H. rp. 176.)

May 1912, p. 748
House, Indian Affairs Committee: Stephens, J. H. Report amending H. 22647, for sale and entry of lands [within lands reserved for Cantonment Indian School on former Cheyenne and Arapaho Reservation], Okla. May 14, 1912. 4 p. (H. rp. 704.)

August 1912, p. 120
Justice Department: Reel, Alexander H. In Court of Claims, Indian depredations, Reel v. United States and Brule and Ogallala Sioux, and Sioux Tribe, Northern Cheyenne and Arapahoe, and Cheyenne and Arapahoe Tribe of Indians. [1912.] 15 p.

November 1912, p. 229
Court of Claims: Sorrell. Charles Sorrell v. United States [and Arapaho Indians]; evidence for claimant. [1912.] no. 78, p. 1-36.

April 1913, p. 558
Court of Claims: Sorrell. Mary Ann Sorrell [widow of Charles Sorrell] v. United States [and Arapaho Indians]; evidence for claimant. [1913.] Indian depredations, no. 78, p. 37-60.

May 1913, p. 624
Justice Department: Sorrell, Charles. Nos. 78 and 461, in Court of Claims, Indian depredations, Sorrell v. United States and Arapaho Indians; [same] v. United States and Shoshone Indians; defendants' request for findings of fact, objections to findings of fact requested by claimant, and brief. 1913. cover-title, p. 1-38.

November 1913, p. 230
Justice Department: Sorrell, Charles. In Court of Claims, Indian depredations, Charles Sorrell v. United States and Arapaho Indians, no. 78; [same] v. United States and Shoshone Indians, no. 461; defendants' supplemental brief. [1913.] p. 1-12.

June 1914, p. 694
Justice Department: Tesson, Joseph. In Court of Claims, Indian depredations, Joseph Tesson v. United States and Sioux Indians, no. 1434   [same] v. United States and Arapahoe Indians, no. 1435; defendants' request for findings of fact, objections to findings of fact requested by claimant, and brief. [1914.] p. 1-11.

April 1915, p. 579
Justice Department: Sorrell, Charles. In Court of Claims, Indian depredations, Charles Sorrell v. United States and Arapaho Indians, no. 78; [same] v. United States and Shoshone Indians, no. 461; defendants' brief. [1915.] p. 1-11.

October 1915, p. 162
Justice Department: Tamney, Michael. In Court of Claims, Indian depredations, B. U. Jamison, administrator [of] Michael Tamney, v. United States and Arapaho Indians, no. 1726; defendants' brief. [1915.] p. 21-29.

January 1916, p. 362
President of United States: Cheyenne and Arapaho Reservation. Executive order [setting aside certain lands in Oklahoma for agency and school purposes in connection with administration of Cheyenne and Arapaho Indian Agency in Oklahoma]. Dec. 29, 1915. 1 p. f° (No. 2294.)

May 1916, p. 694
Justice Department: Guttmann, Friedman & Co. In Court of Claims, Indian depre-
dations, Felipe W. Guttmann, administrator [of] Adolph Guttmann, surviving partner,
Guttmann, Friedman & Company, v. United States and Kiowa, Arapaho, and Comanche
Indians, no. 1898; defendants' brief. [1916.] p. 29-35.

October 1916, p. 235
Justice Department: Dieteman, Apollinaris. In Court of Claims, Indian depredations,
Maria Ida D. Roesch, administratrix [of] Apollinaris Dieteman, v. United States and
Cheyenne and Arapaho Indians, no. 4941; defendants' brief. [1916.] p. 101-107.

October 1916, p. 235
Justice Department: Bachman, Fred. In Court of Claims, Indian depredations, Fred
Bachman, jr., administrator [of] Fred Bachman, v. United States and Sioux, Chey-
enne, and Arapaho Indians, no. 3207; defendants' brief. [1916.] p. 108-109.

October 1916, p. 236
Justice Department: Schindelholz, Anton. In Court of Claims, Indian depredations,
Marie L. Dieteman, executrix [of] Anton Schindelholz, v. United States and Cheyenne
and Arapaho Indians, no. 4939; defendants' brief. [1916.] p. 110-113.

November 1916, p. 288
Justice Department: Smith, Henry. In Court of Claims, William F. Smith, administrator of Henry Smith, v. United States and Cheyenne and Arapaho Indians, no. 6696;
defendants' brief. [1916.] p. 114-115.

January 1917, p. 411
House, Indian Affairs Committee: Cheyenne and Arapaho Reservation. Extension of
time of payment for lands in Cheyenne and Arapahoe Reservations, Okla., report to
accompany H. R. 19785; submitted by Mr. Carter of Oklahoma. Jan. 19, 1917. 2 p.
(H. rp. 1324.)

January 1917, p. 425
Senate, Indian Affairs Committee: Cheyenne and Arapaho Reservation. Extension of
time of payment to purchasers of lands in Cheyenne and Arapahoe Reservation, Okla.,
report to accompany S. 7757; submitted by Mr. Owen. Jan. 9, 1917. 2 p. (S. rp.
908.)

February 1917, p. 497
Public laws, Public [act] 297-350, 64th Congress: Cheyenne and Arapaho Reservation.
S. 7757, act authorizing further extension of time to purchasers of land in former
Cheyenne and Arapahoe Indian Reservation, Okla., within which to make payment.
Approved Feb. 23, 1917. 1 p. (Public 350.)

April 1917, p. 678
President of United States: Indians. Executive order [providing that trust period
on allotments of Cheyenne and Arapaho Indians in Oklahoma, which trust expires during calendar year 1917, be extended for period of 10 years from dates of expiration,
except those named in order]. [Apr. 4, 1917.] [2] p. ([No. 2580.])

April 1920, p. 577
Senate, Indian Affairs Committee: Arapaho Indians. Northern Arapahoe tribe and Nor-
thern Cheyenne tribe of Indians, report to accompany S. 3164 [authorizing Northern
Arapahoe tribe and Northern Cheyenne tribe of Indians to submit claims to Court of
Claims]; submitted by Mr. Curtis. Apr. 22, 1920. 1 p. (S. rp. 534.)

June 1926, p. 1017
House, Indian Affairs Committee: Cheyenne Indians. Permit Cheyenne and Arapahoe
tribes to file suit in Court of Claims, report to accompany H. R. 12533 [to amend
act of June 3, 1920 (41st Statutes at large, p. 738), so as to permit Cheyenne and
Arapahoe tribes to file suit in Court of Claims]; submitted by Mr. Leavitt. June 3,
1926. 2 p. (H. rp. 1361, 69th Cong. 1st sess.)

June 1926, p. 1042
Senate, Indian Affairs Committee: <u>Cheyenne Indians</u>. Permit Cheyenne and Arapahoe
tribes to file suit in Court of Claims, report to accompany S. 4223 [to amend act of
June 3, 1920 (41st Statutes at large, p. 738), so as to permit Cheyenne and Arapahoe
tribes to file suit in Court of Claims]; submitted by Mr. Kendrick.   June 1, 1926.
2 p. (S. rp. 971, 69th Cong. 1st sess.)

July 1926, p. 22
Public laws: Public [act] 410-439½, 441-523, 69th Congress: <u>Cheyenne Indians</u>. S.4223,
act to amend act of June 3, 1920 (41st Statutes at large, p. 738), so as to permit
Cheyenne and Arapahoe tribes to file suit in Court of Claims.   Approved June 24, 1926.
1 p. (Public 421.)

February 1927, p. 641
President of United States: <u>Indians</u>. Executive order [providing that trust period on
allotments of Cheyenne and Arapaho Indians in Oklahoma, which expires during calendar year 1927, be extended for period of 10 years, except those named in order].
Feb. 17, 1927. 1 p. (No. 4587.)

March 1928, p. 681
House, Indian Affairs Committee: <u>Arapaho Indians</u>.   Arapahoe and Cheyenne Indians,
report to accompany H. R. 11359 [for relief of Arapahoe and Cheyenne Indians]; submitted by Mr. Leavitt. Mar. 15, 1928. 2 p. (H. rp. 954, 70th Cong. 1st sess.)

March 1928, p. 714
Senate, Indian Affairs Committee: <u>Arapaho Indians</u>.   Permit Arapahoe and Cheyenne
tribes to file suit in Court of Claims, report to accompany S. 3343; submitted by
Mr. Kendrick. Mar. 6, calendar day Mar. 7, 1928. 3 p. (S. rp. 496, 70th Cong.
1st sess.)

April 1928, p. 800
Public laws, Public [act] 181-288, 70th Congress: <u>Arapaho Indians</u>.   S. 3343, act for
relief of Arapahoe and Cheyenne Indians. Approved Mar. 29, 1928. 1 p. (Public 208.)

April 1928, p. 814
House, Indian Affairs Committee: <u>Arapaho Indians</u>.   Arapahoe and Cheyenne Indians,
hearings, 70th Congress, 1st session, on H. R. 11359 [for relief of Arapahoe and
Cheyenne Indians], Mar. 1 and 15, 1928. 1928. ii + 12 p.

April 1928, p. 815
House, Indian Affairs Committee: <u>Shoshoni Indians</u>.   Per capita payment to Shoshone
and Arapahoe Indians of Wyoming [from funds held in trust for them by United States],
report to accompany H. R. 11365; submitted by Mr. Arentz. Apr. 12, 1928. 2 p.
(H. rp. 1238, 70th Cong. 1st sess.)

April 1928, p. 849
Senate, Indian Affairs Committee: <u>Shoshoni Indians</u>.   Authorizing per capita payment
to Shoshone and Arapahoe Indians of Wyoming [from funds held in trust for them by
United States], report to accompany S. 3366; submitted by Mr. Kendrick. Apr. 9,
calendar day Apr. 12, 1928. 2 p. (S. rp. 789, 70th Cong. 1st sess.)

May 1928, p. 936
Public [act] 289-462, 70th Congress: <u>Shoshoni Indians</u>.   S. 3366, act to authorize
per capita payment to Shoshone and Arapahoe Indians of Wyoming from funds held in
trust for them by United States. Approved Apr. 28, 1928. 1 p. (Public 324.)

March 1930, p. 693
Public laws: Public [act] 53-78, 71st Congress: <u>Shoshoni Indians</u>.   S. 3579, act
authorizing per capita payment to Shoshone and Arapahoe Indians. Approved Mar. 24,
1930. 1 p. (Public 77.)

March 1930, p. 704
House, Indian Affairs Committee: <u>Shoshoni Indians</u>.   Per capita payments to Shoshone
and Arapahoe Indians, report to accompany H. R. 10216; submitted by Mr. Leavitt.
Mar. 12, 1930. 4 p. (H. rp. 886, 71st Cong. 2d sess.)

March 1930, p. 722
Shoshoni Indians. Authorizing per capita payments to Shoshone and Arapahoe Indians,
report to accompany S. 3579; submitted by Mr. Frazier. Jan. 6, calendar day Mar. 8,
1930. 2 p. (S. rp. 261, 71st Cong. 2d sess.)

January 1931, p. 500
House, Indian Affairs Committee: Shoshoni Indians. Additional per capita payment
to Shoshone and Arapahoe Indians, report to accompny S. 5295; submitted by
Mr. Leavitt. Jan. 15, 1931. 2 p. (H. rp. 2274, 71st Cong. 3d sess.)

January 1931, p. 522
Senate, Indian Affairs Committee: Shoshoni Indians. Authorizing per capita payment
to Shoshone and Arapahoe Indians, report to accompany S. 5295 [authorizing additional per capita payment to Shoshone and Arapahoe Indians]; submitted by Mr. Kendrick.
Jan. 5, calendar day Jan. 7, 1931. 1 p. (S. rp. 1244, 71st Cont. 3d sess.)

February 1931, p. 619
Public [act] 568-672, 71st Congress: Shoshoni Indians. S. 5295, act authorizing
additional per capita payment to Shoshone and Arapahoe Indians. Approved Feb. 3,
1931. 1 p.

April 1935, p. 394
Senate, Indian Affairs Committee: Arapaho Indians. Arapahoe and Cheyenne jurisdictional bill, report to accompany S. 1504 [authorizing Arapahoe and Cheyenne
Indians to submit claims to Court of Claims]; submitted by Mr. Wheeler. Apr. 11,
1935. 4 p. (S. rp. 465, 74th Cong. 1st sess.)

June 1935, p. 642
House, Indian Affairs Committee: Arapaho Indians. Claims of Arapahoe and Cheyenne
Indians, report to accompany S. 1504 [authorizing Arapahoe and Cheyenne Indians
to submit claims to Court of Claims]; submitted by Mr. Ayers. June 3, 1935. 2 p.
(H. rp. 1091, 74th Cong. 1st sess.)

April 1937, p. 442
Senate, Indian Affairs Committee: Arapaho Indians. Arapahoe and Cheyenne jurisdictional bill, report to accompany S. 1622 [authorizing Arapahoe and Cheyenne
Indians to submit claims to Court of Claims]; submitted by Mr. Wheeler. Mar. 29,
calendar day Apr. 5, 1937. 8 p. (S. rp. 291, 75th Cong. 1st sess.)

July 1937, p. 871
House, Indian Affairs Committee: Arapaho Indians. Arapahoe and Cheyenne jurisdictional bill, report to accompany S. 1622 [authorizing Arapahoe and Cheyenne Indians to submit claims to Court of Claims]; submitted by Mr. O'Connor [of Montana].
July 23, 1937. 5 p. (H. rp. 1293, 75th Cong. 1st sess.)

July 1937, p. 897
Senate, Indian Affairs Committee: Seger School. Eliminating [part of] Seger School
reserve and setting it aside for use of Cheyenne and Arapahoe Indians of Oklahoma,
report to accompany S. 2698; submitted by Mr. Thomas of Oklahoma. July 22, calendar day July 28, 1937, 2 p. (S. rp. 986, 75th Cong. 1st sess.)

March 1938, p. 305
House, Indian Affairs Committee: Seger School. Eliminating [part of] Seger School
reserve and setting it aside for use of Cheyenne and Arapaho Indians of Oklahoma,
report to accompany H. R. 7776; submitted by Mr. Rogers of Oklahoma. Mar. 9, 1938.
4 p. (H. rp. 1922, 75th Cong. 3d sess.)

April 1938, p. 456
Public laws: Public [act] 454-495, 75th Congress: Seger School. S. 2698, act to set
aside lands in Oklahoma for Cheyenne and Arapahoe Indians. Approved Apr. 13, 1938.
1 p. (Public 480.) [The lands to be set aside are part of the Seger School reserve.]

April 1938, p. 497
Interior Department, Indian Affairs Office: Cheyenne Indians. Constitution and by-
laws of Cheyenne-Arapaho Tribes of Oklahoma; ratified Sept. 18, 1937. 1938. [1] +
5 p.

February 1939, p. 182
Senate, Indian Affairs Committee: <u>Arapaho Indians</u>. Arapahoe and Cheyenne jurisdictional bill, report to accompany S. 864 [authorizing Arapahoe and Cheyenne Indians to submit claims to Court of Claims]; submitted by Mr. Wheeler. Feb. 24, 1939.
9 p. (S. rp. 100, 76th Cong. 1st sess.)

August 1939, p. 1151
House, Indian Affairs Committee: <u>Arapaho Indians</u>. Arapahoe and Cheyenne Indians
jurisdictional act, hearings, 76th Congress, 1st session, on H. R. 2775, authorizing
Arapahoe and Cheyenne Indians to submit claims to Court of Claims, June 20, 1939.
1939. iii + 37 p.

October 1940, p. 1465
House, Indian Affairs Committee: <u>Arapaho Indians</u>. Arapahoe and Cheyenne Indians
jurisdictional act, hearings, 76th Congress, 3d session, on H. R. 2775, authorizing
Arapahoe and Cheyenne Indians to submit claims to Court of Claims, Feb. 21, 1940.
1940. pt. 2, iii + 39-82 p.

June 1941, p. 818
House, Indian Affairs Committee: <u>Arapaho Indians</u>. Arapahoe and Cheyenne juris-
dictional bill, report to accompany H. R. 1065 [authorizing Arapahoe and Cheyenne
Indians or any band thereof to submit their claims against the United States to
Court of Claims]; submitted by Mr. O'Connor. June 12, 1941. 10 p. (H. rp. 764,
77th Cong. 1st sess.) [Includes minority views signed by Fred C. Gilchrist.]

June 1941, p. 834
Senate, Indian Affairs Committee: <u>Arapaho Indians</u>. Arapahoe and Cheyenne jurisdictional bill, report to accompany S. 271 [authorizing Arapahoe and Cheyenne Indians or any band thereof to submit their claims against United States to Court
of Claims]; submitted by Mr. Wheeler. June 19, legislative day June 10, 1941.
15 p. (S. rp. 460, 77th Cong. 1st sess.)

July 1941, p. 987
House, Indian Affairs Committee: <u>Cheyenne-Arapaho Indians</u>, Oklahoma, set aside
lands, report to accompany H. R. 5095 [to set aside lands in Oklahoma for Cheyenne-
Arapaho Tribes of Indians]; submitted by Mr. Rogers of Oklahoma. July 3, 1941. 2 p.
(H. rp. 896, 77th Cong. 1st sess.)

Dec. 1941, p. 1746
Senate, Indian Affairs Committee: <u>Cheyenne Indians</u>. Cheyenne-Arapaho Indians,
Oklahoma, vesting title to lands, and providing for refund of income taxes erroneously paid by certain Indians, report to accompany H. R. 5095 [to set aside lands in
Oklahoma for Cheyenne-Arapaho Tribes of Indians, and to carry out certain obligations to certain enrolled Indians under tribal agreement]; submitted by Mr. Thomas
of Oklahoma. Dec. 4, 1941. 4 p. (S. rp. 856, 77th Cong. 1st sess.)

March 1942, p. 180
Public law 415-455, 77th Congress: <u>Cheyenne Indians</u>. H. R. 5095, act to set aside
lands in Oklahoma for Cheyenne-Arapaho Tribes of Indians, and to carry out certain
obligations to certain enrolled Indians under tribal agreement [by providing for
refund of income taxes erroneously paid by Indians]. [Approved Jan. 29, 1942.]
2 p. (Public law 419.)

April 1943, p. 439
Senate, Indian Affairs Committee: <u>Arapaho Indians</u>. Arapahoe and Cheyenne jurisdictional bill, report to accompany S. 409 [authorizing Arapahoe and Cheyenne
Indians or any band thereof to submit their claims against United States to Court
of Claims]; submitted by Mr. Wheeler, Mar. 5, 1943. 15 p. (S. rp. 86, 78th Cong.
1st sess.)

April 1943, p. 453
Interior Department, Indian Affairs Office: <u>Cheyenne Indians</u>. Amendment to Consti-
tution and by-laws of Cheyenne-Arapaho Tribes of Oklahoma; [approval recommended
Nov. 6, 1941]. [1943.] 2 leaves.

April 1947, p. 385
House, Public Lands Committee: <u>Shoshone Indians</u>. Authorizing segregation and ex-
penditure of trust funds held in joint ownership by Shoshone and Arapaho tribes of
Wind River Reservation, report to accompany H. R. 1098; submitted by Mr. Welch.
Mar. 20, 1947. 4 p. (H. rp. 172, 80th Cong. 1st sess.)

May 1947, p. 518
Senate, Pubic Lands Committee: <u>Shoshone Indians</u>. Providing for payment to each enrolled member of Shoshone and Arapahoe tribes of Wind River Reservation, Wyo., from
joint funds standing to their credit in Treasury, report to accompany S. 666 [to
authorize segregation and expenditure of trust funds held in joint ownership by
Shoshone and Arapaho tribes of Wind River Reservation]; submitted by Mr. Robertson
of Wyoming. Apr. 21, 1947. 4 p. (S. rp. 117, 80th Cong. 1st sess.)

June 1947, p. 663
House, Public Lands Committee: <u>Shoshone Indians</u>. Trust funds, Shoshone and Arapaho
Indian tribes, hearings before subcommittee on Indian affairs, 80th Congress,
1st session, on H. R. 1098, to authorize segregation and expenditure of trust
funds held in joint ownership by Shoshone and Arapaho tribes of Wind River Reservation, Mar. 15, 1947. 1947. iii + 40 p. (Committee hearing no. 6.)

July 1947, p. 797
Public law 47-86, 80th Congress: <u>Shoshone Indians</u>. H. R. 1098, act to authorize
segregation and expenditure of trust funds held in joint ownership by Shoshone and
Arapaho tribes of Wind River Reservation. [Approved May 19, 1947.] 2 p. (Public
law 74, 80th Congress. Chapter 80, 1st session.)

August 1951, p. 37
Senate reports, 82d Congress: 13501--541. Per capita payments to members of Sho-
shone and Arapaho tribes, Wyoming. Report from Committee on Interior and Insular
Affairs to accompany S. 950. July 11, 1951. 3 p.

September 1951, p. 28
House reports, 82d Congress: 14964--863. Per capita payments to members of Shoshone
and Arapaho tribes, Wyoming. Report from Committee on Interior and Insular Affairs
to accompany S. 950. Aug. 14, 1951. 3 p.

October 1951, p. 18
Public laws, 82d Congress: 16339--133. S. 950, to act to amend act authorizing
segregation and expenditure of trust funds held in joint ownership by Shoshone and
Arapaho tribes of Wind River Reservation for purpose of extending time in which
payments are to be made to members of such tribes under such act, and for other
purposes. Approved Aug. 30, 1951. 1 p. (Chapter 367, 1st session.)

June 1952, p. 29
House reports, 82d Congress: 8863--1935. Setting aside certain lands in Oklahoma,
formerly part of Cheyenne-Arapaho Reservation, and known as Fort Reno military
reservation, for Cheyenne-Arapaho Tribes of Indians of Oklahoma. Report from Committee on Interior and Insular Affairs to accompany H. R. 1631. May 16, 1952. 8 p.

July 1952, p. 38
House, Interior and Insular Affairs Committee [Committee hearings serials], 82d Congress: 10637--14. Lands on Fort Reno military reservation, Okla., hearings before
subcommittee on Indian affairs, 82d Congress, 2d session, on H. R. 1631, Mar. 4-
Apr. 5, 1952. 1952. iii + 48 p.

August 1952, p. 33
Public laws, 82d Congress: 13167--591. S. 3333, act to vest title in United States
to certain lands and interests in lands of Shoshone and Arapaho Indian tribes of
Wind River Reservation and to provide compensation therefor and for other purposes.
Approved July 18, 1952. 1 p. (Chapter 946, 2d session.)

August 1952, p. 54
Senate reports: 13713--1980. Boysen Dam acquisition of lands which are subject to
certain rights of Shoshone and Arapaho Indian tribes of Wind River Reservation, Wyo.
Report from Committee on Interior and Insular Affairs to accompany S. 3333. June 27,
1952. 54 p.

May 1953, p. 38
House reports, 83d Congress: 7390--261. Amending act of May 19, 1947, so as to in-
crease percentage of certain trust funds held by Shoshone and Arapaho tribes of Wind
River Reservation which is to be distributed per capita to individual members of
such tribes. Report from Committee on Interior and Insular Affairs to accompany
H. R. 444. Apr. 13, 1953. 3 p.

May 1953, p. 38
House reports, 83d Congress: 7398--269. Providing compensation to Shoshone and
Arapahoe tribes of Indians for certain lands of Riverton reclamation project within
ceded portion of Wind River Indian Reservation. Report from Committee on Interior
and Insular Affairs to accompany H. R. 4483. Apr. 14, 1953. 4 p.

June 1953, p. 39
Senate reports, 82d Congress: 9126--263. Per capita distribution, Shoshone and
Arapaho tribes, Wyoming. Report from Committee on Interior and Insular Affairs to
accompany H. R. 444. May 12, 1953. 4 p.

August 1953, p. 54
Senate reports, 83d Congress: 12910--644. Compensation to Shoshone and Arapahoe
Tribes of Indians for certain lands of Riverton reclamation project, Wyo. Report
from Committee on Interior and Insular Affairs to accompany H. R. 4483. July 28,
1953. 11 p.

September 1953, p. 30
Public laws, 83d Congress: 15199--132. H. R. 444, act to amend act of May 19, 1947,
so as to increase percentage of certain trust funds held by Shoshone and Arapaho
Tribes of Wind River Reservation which is to be distributed per capita to individual
members of such tribes. Approved July 17, 1953. 1 p. (Chapter 223, 1st session.)

September 1953, p. 35
Public laws, 83d Congress: 15337--284. H. R. 4483, act to provide compensation to
Shoshone and Arapahoe Tribes of Indians for certain lands of Riverton reclamation
project within ceded portion of Wind River Reservation and for other purposes.
[Approved Aug. 15, 1953.] 22 p. (Chapter 509, 1st session.)

September 1955, p. 38
Public laws, 84th Congress: 14444--278. S. 2087, act to amend act of May 19, 1947
(ch. 80, 61 Stat. 102), as amended, so as to permit per capita payments to individual members of Shoshone Tribe and Arapahoe Tribe of Wind River Reservation in
Wyoming, to be made quarterly. Approved Aug. 9, 1955. 1 p. (Chapter 638, 1st session.)

September 1955, p. 53
House reports on public bills, 84th Congress: 14854--1486. Amending act of May 19,
1947 (ch. 80, 61 stat. 102) as amended so as to permit per capita payments to individual members of Shoshone Tribe and Arapahoe Tribe of Wind River Reservation in
Wyoming to be made quarterly. Report from Committee on Interior and Insular Affairs to accompany H. R. 6945. July 27, 1955. 3 p.

September 1955, p. 73
Senate reports on public bills, 84th Congress: 15379--1168. Amending act of
May 19, 1947 (ch. 80, 61 Stat. 102), as amended, so as to permit per capita payments
to individual members of Shoshone Tribe and Arapahoe Tribe of Wind River Reservation
in Wyoming, to be made quarterly. Report from Committee on Interior and Insular
Affairs to accompany S. 2087. July 27, 1955. 3 p.

August 1956, p. 45
Senate reports on public bills, 84th Congress: 12301--2231. Authorizing conveyance
of tribal lands from Shoshone Indian tribe and Arapahoe Indian tribe of Wind River
Reservation in Wyoming to United States. Report from Committee on Interior and
Insular Affairs to accompany S. 3467. June 14, 1956. 7 p.

August 1956, p. 48
Senate reports on public bills, 84th Congress: 12376--2369. Amending sec. 3 of act
of May 9, 1947 (ch. 80, 61 Stat. 102), as amended, for purpose of extending time
in which payments are to be made to members of Shoshone Tribe and Arapahoe Tribe of
Wind River Reservation in Wyoming. Report from Committee on Interior and Insular
Affairs to accompany S. 3397. June 26, 1956. 11 p.

September 1956, p. 33
Public laws, 84th Congress: 14555--794. S. 3397, act to amend sec. 3 of Act of
May 19, 1947 (ch. 80, 61 Stat. 102), as amended, for purpose of extending time in
which payments are to be made to members of Shoshone Tribe and Arapahoe Tribe of
Wind River Reservation in Wyoming, and for other purposes. Approved July 25, 1956.
1 p. (Chapter 723, 2d session.)

September 1956, p. 41
House reports on public bills, 84th Congress: 14734--2592. Amending sec. 3 of act
of May 19, 1947 (Ch. 80, 61 stat. 102), as amended for purpose of extending time in
which payments are to be made to members of Shoshone Tribe and Arapahoe Tribe of
Wind River Reservation in Wyoming. July 3, 1956. 12 p. Report from Committee on
Interior and Insular Affairs to accompany H. R. 11928.

September 1956, p. 43
House reports on public bills, 84th Congress: 14811--2706. Authorizing conveyance
of tribal lands from Shoshone Indian tribe and Arapahoe Indian Tribe of Wind River
Reservation in Wyoming to United States. Report from Committee on Interior and
Insular Affairs to accompany H. R. 10183. July 12, 1956. 8 p.

September 1956, p. 49
House reports on public bills, 84th Congress: 14974--2956. Conveyance of tribal
lands. Conference report to accompany S. 3467. July 27, 1956. 3 p.

October 1956, p. 33
Public laws, 84th Congress: 16829--960. S. 3467, act to authorize conveyance of
tribal lands from Shoshone Indian tribe and Arapahoe Indian tribe of Wind River
Reservation in Wyoming to United States. [Approved Aug. 3, 1956.] 2 p. (Chapter 931, 2d session.)

June 1958, p. 24
House reports on public bills, 85th Congress: 6815--1666. Setting aside certain
lands in Oklahoma for Cheyenne and Arapaho Indians. Report from Committee on Interior and Insular Affairs to accompany H. R. 6090. Apr. 29, 1958. 5 p.

July 1958, p. 30
House reports on public bills, 85th Congress: 8261--1842. Amending sec. 2 and 3
of act of May 19, 1947, as amended, relating to trust funds of Shoshone and
Arapahoe tribes. Report from Committee on Interior and Insular Affairs to accompany H. R. 12617. June 2, 1958. 9 p.

August 1958, p. 35
Senate reports on public bills, 85th Congress: 9708--1746. Relating to minerals of
Wind River Indian Reservation in Wyoming. Report from Committee on Interior and
Insular Affairs to accompany S. 3202. June 24, 1958. 7 p.

September 1958, p. 33
Public laws, 85th Congress: 11806--610. H. R. 12617, act to amend sec. 2 and 3 of
act of May 19, 1947 (ch. 80, 61 Stat. 102) as amended, relating to trust funds of
Shoshone and Arapahoe Tribes and for other purposes. [Approved Aug. 8, 1958.] 2 p.

September 1958, p. 45
House reports on public bills, 85th Congress: 12143--2453. Relating to minerals on
Wind River Indian Reservation in Wyoming. Report from Committee on Interior and
Insular Affairs to accompany S. 3203. Aug. 5, 1958. 6 p.

September 1958, p. 58
Senate reports on public bills, 85th Congress: 12450--1869. Amending sec. 2 and 3
of act of May 19, 1947 (ch. 80, 61 Stat. 102), as amended, relating to trust funds
of Shoshone and Arapahoe Tribes. Report from Committee on Interior and Insular Affairs to accompany H. R. 12617. July 22, 1958. 9 p.

October 1958, p. 36
Public laws, 85th Congress: 14125--780. S. 3203, act relating to minerals on Wind
River Indian Reservation in Wyoming, and for other purposes. [Approved, Aug. 27,
1958.] 2 p.

October 1958, p. 63
Senate reports on public bills, 85th Congress: 14796--2335. Conveying certain lands
in Oklahoma for Cheyenne and Arapaho Indians. Report from Committee on Interior
and Insular Affairs to accompany H. R. 6090. Aug. 12, 1958. 4 p.

July 1959, p. 23
House reports on public bills, 86th Congress: 8642--378. Setting aside certain
lands in Oklahoma for Cheyenne and Arapaho Indians. Report from Committee on Interior and Insular Affairs to accompany H. R. 816. May 25, 1959. 5 p.

October 1959, p. 38
Senate reports on public bills, 86th Congress: 14443--654. Placing in trust status
certain lands on Wind River Indian Reservation in Wyoming. Report from Committee
on Interior and Insular Affairs to accompany S. 1751. Aug. 11, 1959. 3 p.

May 1960, p. 26
House reports on public bills, 86th Congress: 6606--1486. Placing in trust status
certain lands on Wind River Indian Reservation, Wyo. Report from Committee on Interior and Insular Affairs to accompany H. R. 5870. Apr. 12, 1960. 5 p.

July 1960, p. 19
Public laws, 86th Congress: 9369--450. S. 1751, act to place in trust status certain lands on Wind River Indian Reservation in Wyoming. Approved May 6, 1960. 1 p.

August 1960, p. 35
Senate reports on public bills, 86th Congress: 11125--1617. Setting aside certain
lands in Oklahoma for Cheyenne and Arapaho Indians. Report from Committee on Interior and Insular Affairs to accompany H. R. 816. June 20, 1960. 7 p.

November 1960, p. 25
Public Laws, 86th Congress: 16814--791. H. R. 816, act to convey certain lands in
Oklahoma to Cheyenne and Arapaho Indians, and for other purposes. Approved
Sept. 14, 1960. 1 p.

September 1967, p. 32
Senate reports on public bills, 90th Congress: 13835--456. Declaring that certain
land of United States is held by United States in trust for Cheyenne and Arapaho
Tribes of Oklahoma. Report from Committee on Interior and Insular Affairs to accompany S. 1173. July 28, 1967. 5 p.

October 1967, p. 17
House reports on public bills, 90th Congress: 15007--624. Providing for disposition
of judgment funds now on deposit to credit of Cheyenne-Arapaho Tribes of Oklahoma.
Report from Committee on Interior and Insular Affairs to accompany H. R. 11847.
Aug. 30, 1967. 4 p.

October 1967, p. 24
Senate reports on public bills, 90th Congress: 15118--530. Providing for disposition
of judgment funds now on deposit to credit of Cheyenne-Arapaho Tribes of Oklahoma.
Report from Committee on Interior and Insular Affairs to accompany S. 1933.
Aug. 18, 1967. 12 p.

January 1968, p. 12
Public laws, 90th Congress: 169--117. S. 1933, act to provide for disposition of
judgment funds now on deposit to credit of Cheyenne-Arapaho Tribes of Oklahoma.
[Approved Oct. 31, 1967.] 2 p.

June 1968, p. 24
House reports on public bills, 90th Congress: 7329--1325. Conveying certain federally owned lands to Cheyenne and Arapaho Tribes of Oklahoma. Report from Committee
on Interior and Insular Affairs to accompany S. 1173. Apr. 29, 1968. 3 p.

August 1968, p. 21
Public laws, 90th Congress: 10174--310. S. 1173, act to convey certain federally
owned lands to Cheyenne and Arapaho Tribes of Oklahoma. Approved May 18, 1968. 1 p.

October 1968, p. 19
House documents, 90th Congress: 13835--266. Compilation of....laws....and related
enactments through Jan. 2, 1968. v. 1. ix + 1-480 + xxxiv p.; v. 2. ix + 481-975
+ xxxiv p.

September 1972, p. 18
House reports on public bills, 92d Congress: 11807--1075. Amending act entitled
Act to provide for disposition of judgment funds now on deposit to credit of Cheyenne-Arapaho Tribes of Oklahoma, approved Oct. 31, 1967 (81 Stat. 337). Report
from Committee on Interior and Insular Affairs to accompany H. R. 6575. May 22, 1972.
4 p.

March 1973, p. 16
Public laws, 92d Congress, 1st session: 19374--439. H. R. 6575, act to amend act
entitled Act to provide for disposition of judgment funds now on deposit to credit
of Cheyenne-Arapaho Tribes of Oklahoma, approved Oct. 31, 1967 (81 Stat. 337). Approved Sept. 29, 1972. 1 p.

November 1973, p. 51
General information: 31447--Indians: Arapahos [with suggested reading list]. [Aug.
1966.] 3 p.

January 1975, p. 20
Senate reports on public bills, 93d Congress: 00333--862. Declaring that certain
land of United States is held by United States in trust for Cheyenne-Arapaho Tribes
of Aklahoma [Oklahoma]. Report from Committee on Interior and Insular Affairs to
accompany S. 521. May 21, 1974. 3 p.

March 1975, p. 18
House reports on public bills, 93d Congress: 03602--1583. Declaring that certain
land of United States is held by United States in trust for Cheyenne-Arapaho Tribes
of Oklahoma. Report from Committee on Interior and Insular Affairs to accompany
H. R. 3605. Dec. 13, 1974. 3 p.

April 1975, p. 22
Public laws, 93d Congress: 05037--582. S. 521, act to declare that certain land of
United States is held by United States in trust for Cheyenne-Arapaho Tribes of Okla-
homa. Approved Jan. 2, 1975. 1 p.

November 1977, p. 257
United States Congress, Senate, Select Committee on Indian Affairs: Cheyenne-Arapaho
land conveyance: report to accompany S. 1291.--[Washington: U.S. Govt. Print. Off.,
1977]. 7 p.; 24 cm.--(Senate report - 95th Congress, 1st session; no. 95-239).
77-15878.

October 1978, p. 517
95-2: H. rp. 1306. United States Congress, House, Committee on Interior and Insular
Affairs. Declaring that certain lands of the United States situated in the State
of Oklahoma are held by the United States in trust for the Cheyenne-Arapaho Tribes
of Oklahoma...: report to accompany S. 1291.--[Washington: U.S. Govt. Print. Off.,
1978]. 5p.; 24 cm.--(House report - 95th Congress, 2d session; no. 95-1306).
78-22601.

December 1978, p. 335
95-2: Pub. Law 327. United States, Laws, statutes, etc. An act to declare that certain lands of the United States situated in the State of Oklahoma are held by the
United States in trust for the Cheyenne-Arapaho Tribes of Oklahoma, and to authorize
the Secretary of the Interior to accept conveyance from the Cheyenne-Arapaho Tribes
of Oklahoma of certain other lands in Oklahoma to be held in trust by the United
States for such tribes.--[Washington: for sale by the Supt. of Docs., U.S. Govt.
Print. Off., 1978]. 20402. [2] p.; 24 cm.--(Public Law; 95-327). 78-27012.

E

United States Statutes at Large

The following is a listing of pages on which the Arapaho Indians are referred to in the multivolume United States Statutes at Large (in part also titled Statutes at Large...of the United States of America), the published record of all federal laws and resolutions, public and private, as enacted, as well as of all executive proclamations issued during congressional sessions. The entries are arranged chronologically by volume, and list the part (if applicable), year of publication (in parentheses), and page(s) on which the references may be found; references to treaties are so indicated.

Volume 11 (1859), p. 749 (Treaty of Fort Laramie of September 17, 1851)

Volume 12 (1863), pp. 59, 528-9, 791, and 1163-9 (Treaty of February 18, 1861, at Fort Wise)

Volume 13 (1866), pp. 176 and 555-6

Volume 14 (1868), pp. 271, 276, 493, 703-11 (Treaty of October 14, 1865, at Little Arkansas River), and 713-5 (Treaty of October 17, 1865)

Volume 15 (1869), pp. 200, 593-9 (Treaty of October 28, 1867, at Council Camp), 635-47 (Treaty of Fort Laramie of April 29 et seq., 1868), and 655-9 (Treaty of Fort Laramie of May 10, 1868)

Volume 16 (1871), pp. 15-6, 336, 347, 546, and 556-7

Volume 17 (1873), pp. 10, 166-7, 177, 190, 440-1, and 450

Volume 18, Part 3 (1875), pp. 141, 149-50, 423, 434, and 448

Volume 19 (1877), pp. 178, 186, 195, 254-264, 273, 281, and 290

Volume 20 (1879), pp. 67, 74, 84, 298, 304, 313, and 414

Volume 21 (1881), pp. 64, 67, 117, 122, 422, 487, 492, and 498

Volume 22 (1883), pp. 9, 47, 71, 75, 82, 86-7, 265, 435, and 445

Volume 23 (1885), pp. 78, 89, 95, 364, 369, 377, and 498

Volume 24 (1887), pp. 30-1, 41, 293, 300, 450-1, and 460

Volume 25 (1889), pp. 218-9, 230, 981, 983, and 994

Volume 26 (1891), pp. 337-8, 343, 350, 352, 549, 989-91, 992, 996, 1004, 1022, and 1025

Volume 27 (1893), pp. 122-3, 128, 134-5, 138, 613, 615, 619, 627-8, and 1018

Volume 28 (1895), pp. 3, 286, 289, 294, 302-3, 873, 876, 879, 883, 891-2, and 901

Volume 29 (1897), pp. 321, 325, 329, and 336

Volume 30 (1899), pp. 63, 66, 70, 77, 93-4, 96, 571, 579, 581, 584, 924, 931, 934, and 937-8

Volume 31 (1901), pp. 221, 228, 231, 234, 301, 1058, 1065, 1069, and 1071

Volume 32, Part 1 (1903), pp. 251, 253, 255, 987, and 991

Volume 33, Part 1 (1905), pp. 197, 202, 1016, 1052, and 1057

Volume 34, Part 1 (1907), pp. 354, 362, 1035, and 1043

Volume 35, Part 1 (1909), pp. 84, 88, 797, and 802

Volume 36, Part 1 (1911), pp. 190, 277, 280, 1066, and 1096

Volume 37, Part 1 (1913), pp. 527 and 529

Volume 38, Part 1 (1915), pp. 90-1, 93, 230, 593, and 596

Volume 39, Part 1 (1917), pp. 31, 139, 145, 980, and 982

Volume 40, Part 1 (1919), pp. 574 and 577

Volume 41, Part 1 (1921), pp. 16, 20, 31, 421, 425, 434, 1237, and 1240

Volume 42, Part 1 (1923), pp. 571, 574, 1165, 1192, and 1195

Volume 43, Part 1 (1925), pp. 409, 411, 708, 1160-1, and 1329

Volume 44, Part 1 (1927), pp. 473-4, 764, 952, and 954

Volume 45, Part 1 (1929), pp. 47, 222-3, 380, 467, 1583, and 1617

Volume 46, Part 1 (1931), pp. 88, 300-1, 1060, and 1137-8

Volume 52 (1938), p. 213

Volume 58, Part 1 (1945), p. 482

Volume 59, Part 1 (1946), p. 336

Volume 60, Part 1 (1947), pp. 357 and 361

Volume 61, Part 1 (1948), p. 102

Volume 65 (1952), p. 208

Volume 66 (1953), p. 780

Volume 67 (1953), pp. 179 and 592

Volume 69 (1955), p. 557

Volume 70 (1957), pp. 642 and 987

Volume 72 (1959), p. 541

Volume 81 (1968), p. 337

Volume 82 (1969), pp. 124 and 131

Volume 86 (1973), p. 742

Volume 88, Part 2 (1976), p. 1915

Volume 92 (1980), p. 407

Archives and Museums
Possessing Significant Collections
Pertaining to the
Arapaho Indians

F

Archives with Significant Collections of Materials Concerning the Arapaho

The following information was obtained by writing to institutions known to or likely to have in their holdings manuscripts or other documentation, such as recordings of music or photographs, that throw light on the culture of the Arapaho and their relations with other Native Americans, with non-Indians, and especially with the United States government. Even though every effort was made to include all major sources of archival materials, no claim can be made that the listing below is complete.

The list of institutions is arranged alphabetically by locality, with the nature of relevant holdings summarized in a short paragraph. As a rule, more detailed descriptions may be had from archivists upon request.

Bloomington, IN: Archives of Traditional Music, Indiana University, Morrison Hall, Bloomington, IN 47405-2501.
Holdings include fairly extensive recordings of Arapaho music obtained by Zdenek Salzmann in Wyoming in 1949 and 1950 and by Bruno Nettl on the Indiana University campus in 1952.

Bloomington, IN: William Hammond Mathers Museum, Indiana University, 416 North Indiana Avenue, Bloomington, IN 47405.
Holdings include four photographs from about 1880 and 24 images from 1913.

Boulder, CO: Library, University of Colorado, Campus Box 184, Boulder, CO 80309.
Holdings include various collections, including Bent-Hyde Papers, a manuscript by George Bent, and pamphlet files.

Cheyenne, WY: State Historic Preservation Office, Wyoming State Archives, Museums and Historical Department, Barrett Building, Cheyenne, WY 82002.
Holdings include newspaper clippings and several manuscripts pertaining to the Arapaho Indians.

Chicago, IL: Field Museum of Natural History, Roosevelt Road at Lake Shore Drive, Chicago, IL 60605.
Holdings include many manuscript notes pertaining to fieldwork among the Arapaho by George A. Dorsey and Cleaver Warden, as well as black-and-white drawings and watercolors of Arapaho artifacts prepared by a professional illustrator.

Chicago, IL: The Newberry Library, Center for the History of the American Indian, 60 West Walton Street, Chicago, IL 60610.
Holdings include Papers of Richard I. Dodge (1875-) containing a manuscript diary of the Powder River Winter Campaign, various items in the Ayer Collection, miscellaneous materials with linguistic data, and several works of both fiction and nonfiction.

Colorado Springs, CO: Pioneers' Museum, 215 South Tejon Street, Colorado Springs, CO 80903.
Holdings include 28 notebooks of the F. W. Cragin Collection.

Concho, OK: Bureau of Indian Affairs, Concho Agency, Concho, OK 73022.
Holdings include records of several councils of the Cheyenne-Arapaho Business Committee.

Denver, CO: Colorado Historical Society, Colorado State Museum, 1300 Broadway,
Denver, CO 80203.
Holdings contain Dawson Scrapbooks, three oral histories, historical photographs,
and a variety of manuscripts.

Denver, CO: Denver Public Library, 1357 Broadway, Denver, CO 80203-2165.
Holdings include George Bent letters to George Hyde and other materials pertaining
to the early history of the present-day state of Colorado and surrounding areas.

Denver, CO: Division of State Archives and Public Records, Colorado State Department
of Administration, 1313 Sherman Street, Denver, CO 80203.
Holdings include the John Evans Collection pertaining to Indian affairs.

Denver, CO: Federal Records Center, National Archives and Records Administration,
Denver Federal Center, Denver, CO 80225.
Holdings include records of the Bureau of Indian Affairs (Record Group 75), Wind
River Agency, 1920-1980.

Denver, CO: National Archives--Denver Branch, P.O. Box 25307, Denver, CO 80225.
Holdings include records of the Bureau of Indian Affairs (Record Group 75), Wind
River Agency, 1891-1957, containing administrative correspondence, annual reports,
tribal population counts (1895-1907), Arapaho "Family History" (1925), and materials
pertaining to land allotment sale and lease, farming, grazing, irrigation, agricultural extension, soil conservation, Indian health, education and welfare programs,
and the like.

El Reno, OK: El Reno Carnegie Library, 215 East Wade Street, El Reno, OK 73036.
Holdings include letterbooks of the Cheyenne and Arapaho Agency.

Fort Washakie, WY: Wind River Indian Agency, Bureau of Indian Affairs, U.S. Department of the Interior, Fort Washakie, WY 82514.
Holdings include minutes of council meetings, Nell Scott Papers, personnel files,
and other administrative documents on the agency level.

Fort Worth, TX: National Archives--Fort Worth Branch. P.O. Box 6216, Fort Worth,
TX 76115.
Holdings include records relating to Cheyenne and Arapaho Indians of the Concho Indian Agency and School, the bulk falling between 1900 and 1950, with only a few
records of the Seger, Red Moon, and Cantonment agencies and schools that preceded
the Concho Agency (Record Group 75). The agency records concern administration of
Indian lands, heirship proceedings, annuity payrolls, tribal censuses, and vital
statistics. School records include administrative correspondence, student lists,
attendance registers, and the like, falling between 1925 and 1964.

Kansas City, MO: Federal Records Center, National Archives and Records Administration, 2312 East Bannister Road, Kansas City, MO 64131.
Holdings include some of the microfilm records of documents deposited in the National Archives in Washington, DC.

Lander, WY: Fremont County Library, Lander Headquarters, 451 North Second Street,
Lander, WY 82520.
Holdings include materials relating to the history of relations between the Arapaho
and the town and region.

Laramie, WY: Archives of the Episcopal Diocese of Wyoming, 104 South 4th Street,
P.O. Box 1007, Laramie, WY 82070.
Holdings contain correspondence and other miscellaneous materials pertaining to the
missionary work begun by the Protestant Episcopal Church of America among the Arapaho Indians of the Wind River Reservation in Wyoming in 1873.

Laramie, WY: Coe Library, University of Wyoming, Laramie, WY 82071-3412.
Holdings include materials housed in the Archives-American Heritage Center, namely,
Lon L. Newton Papers, Reverend John Roberts Papers (1882-1945), Tacetta Walker
Papers (1860-1930), Francis Donaldson Papers (1872-1950), The Episcopal Church of
Wyoming Collection (1872-1972), and in the Special Collection of the Coe Library the
Salzmann Collection of Materials Concerning the Arapaho Indians, consisting of over
700 articles or book excerpts dealing with the Southern and Northern Arapaho, over
100 cassette tapes of Arapaho language (1981-1983), 15 reel-to-reel tapes with
Arapaho music and language (1949-1952), Salzmann's field notes (1949-1952), English-
Arapaho dictionary cards, and miscellaneous manuscripts by Salzmann, as well as
various materials and tapes concerning the Gros Ventre (Atsina), a group closely related to the Arapaho Indians.

Lincoln, NE: Nebraska State Historical Society, 1500 R Street, Lincoln, NE 68508.
Holdings contain microfilm records of letters received between 1871 and 1872 by the
U.S. Office of the Adjutant General; the correspondence relates in part to the
Arapaho Indians.

Los Angeles, CA: Southwest Museum, P.O. Box 128, Los Angeles, CA 90042.
Holdings include over 30 phonographic cylinders containing Cheyenne and Arapaho music recorded by Frances Densmore in 1935, and numerous photographs and other printed
memorabilia.

Milwaukee, WI: Memorial Library, Marquette University, 1415 West Wisconsin Avenue,
Milwaukee, WI 53233.
Holdings include records of the Bureau of Catholic Indian Missions in both Oklahoma
and Wyoming pertaining to missions as well as schools.

New Haven, CT: The Beinecke Rare Book and Manuscript Library, Yale University,
1603A Yale Station, New Haven, CT 06520.
The most significant source of information concerning the Arapaho Indians in this
library is the Bent Papers, consisting of 260 letters (717 pp.) written by George
Bent (1843-1918) to George E. Hyde between 1904 and 1918 and containing personal
reminiscences of life with the Cheyenne and Arapaho Indians of the Arkansas and
Platte valleys as source material for a book.

New York, NY: American Museum of Natural History, Department of Anthropology, Central Park West at 79th Street, New York, NY 10024.
Holdings contain correspondence relating to A. L. Kroeber's fieldwork among the
Arapaho and five sketches of Arapaho sun dance body paintings collected by Kroeber
but unpublished.

Norman, OK: Library, University of Oklahoma, Norman, OK 73019.
Holdings include The Doris Duke Indian Oral History Collection and various manuscripts pertaining to the Indians of Oklahoma.

North Newton, KS: Library, Bethel College, P.O. Drawer A, North Newton, KS 67117-
9998.
Holdings include the H. R. Voth Collection.

Oklahoma City, OK: Oklahoma Historical Society, Wiley Post Historical Building,
2100 North Lincoln Boulevard, Oklahoma City, OK 73105.
Holdings include extensive records of the Cheyenne and Arapaho Agency in the Indian
Territory (now Oklahoma) during the period 1869-1933, covering all major subjects
under Indian and government relations such as agents' reports, census and enrollment
records, allotment, land leases and sales, intertribal and military relations, Indian annuity and per capita payments, agency financial and personnel records, and
church and school records. The schools include American or Roe's Indian Institute,
Bacone College, Carlisle Indian School, Chilocco Indian School, Genoa Indian School,
Hampton Institute, and Haskell Institute.

Philadelphia, PA: The Historical Society of Pennsylvania, 1300 Locust Street, Philadelphia, PA 19107.
Holdings include the Indian Rights Association Papers. Both a guide to and a microfilm of the collection are available through University Microfilms International,
300 North Zeeb Road, Ann Arbor, MI 48106.

Riverton, WY: Fremont County Library, Riverton Branch Library, 1330 West Park Street, Riverton, WY 82501.
Holdings include materials relating to the history of the relations between the Arapaho and the town and region.

Saint Stephens, WY: St. Stephen's Indian Mission, St. Stephens, WY 82524.
Holdings contain various materials concerning the work of the St. Stephen's Indian Mission (Jesuit) since its founding in 1884.

San Marino, CA: The Huntington Library, 1151 Oxford Road, San Marino, CA 91108.
Holdings include a vocabulary of Sioux, Cheyenne, and Arapaho words (1868-1871) by Ada Adelaide (Adams) Vogdes, and notes on Indians by Walter Scribner Schuyler from 1876.

Topeka, KS: Kansas State Historical Society, 120 West Tenth, Topeka, KS 66612.
Holdings include a manuscript by Albert Barnitz dated April 1, 1866 (13 pp.), and a diary by Winfield Scott Harvey with an account of his service in the 7th U.S. Cavalry and the Battle of Washita (1868-1870).

Washington, DC: Library, Department of the Interior, Washington, DC 20240.
Holdings include miscellaneous materials relating to the history of the relations between the Arapaho and the United States government, such as minutes of councils, Indian Office reports (1845-1894), records of engagements with Indians, and the like. Some of the materials included in the holdings are listed in the Biographical and Historical Index of American Indians and Persons Involved in Indian Affairs, Volumes 1-8, published in 1966 by G. K. Hall and Company in Boston, MA.

Washington, DC: The Library of Congress, Manuscript Division, Washington, DC 20540.
Holdings include the Hugh L. Scott Papers, with some 40,000 items in the main body of the collection that cover more than half a century of military service from his graduation from West Point in 1876 to his army retirement in 1919, as well as four-teen more years of government service until 1933 as a member of the Board of Indian Commissioners. The Hugh L. Scott Papers were described in the May 1952 issue of Quarterly Journal of Current Acquisitions (vol. 9, no. 3).--The Elizabeth Johnston Reynolds Burt Papers also contain information pertaining to the Arapaho.

Washington, DC: National Anthropological Archives, Smithsonian Institution, Washington, DC 20560.
Holdings include field notes of Sister Inez Hilger, A. L. Kroeber, Truman Michelson, and James Mooney; a report and papers by General Hugh L. Scott; the Ethel Cutler Freeman Papers; several valuable collections of photographs from various sources, including Hilger, Michelson, and Mooney; and a variety of manuscripts and field notes of other individuals.

Washington, DC: National Archives, Washington, DC 20408.
Holdings include the records of the Office of the Adjutant General for the period 1780s-1917 (Record Group 94) and the records of the U.S. Army Continental Commands for the period of 1821-1920 (Record Group 393); records of the U. S. House of Representatives (Record Group 233) House Committee on Interior and Insular Affairs, 1951 to the present (legislative files, general correspondence, petitions and memorials, hearings, and subject files) as well as records of the Committee on Public Lands, 1947-1951, and the Committee on Indian Affairs, 1821-1947; records of committees of the U.S. Senate (Record Group 46), including records of the Senate Committee on Indian Affairs dating from the 16th Congress through the 79th (1819-1947), at which time the jurisdiction over Indian-related affairs was transferred to the Senate Committee on Interior and Insular Affairs; Indian Treaty files, 1789-1870, for most Indian treaties submitted to the Senate for its advice and consent; records of the Office of the Secretary of the Interior (Record Group 48), records of the Bureau of Indian Affairs (Record Group 75), and records of the Indian Claims Commission (Record Group 279)--containing such documentary materials as letters, reports, administrative records, rosters of Indian and non-Indian employees, and the like; and Special Reports of the Board of Indian Commissioners. Also, on microfilm, letters received by the Office of Indian Affairs, 1824-1880 (Record Group 75); superintendents' annual narratives and statistical reports from field jurisdictions of the Bureau of Indian Affairs, 1907-1938 (Record Group 75); and reports of inspection of the field jurisdictions of the Office of Indian Affairs (Record Groups 75 and 48).

West Point, NY: United States Military Academy, Special Collections Division, West Point, NY 10996-1799.
Holdings may include references to the Arapaho Indians in the papers of officers who served in the West, for example, in the diaries of John Gregory Bourke.

Note: Individuals wishing to make use of the vast archival materials relating to American Indians in the National Archives of the United States will be aided by Edward E. Hill's Guide to records in the National Archives of the United States relating to American Indians (Washington, DC: GPO, 1981; xiii + 467 pp.; Library of Congress call number Z1209.2.U5H54). References to the Arapaho are found on pages 63, 64, 76, 86, 131, 133, 140, 147, 154, 192, 225, 235, 237, 239, 240, 243, 245, 253, 254, 257, 310, 314, 319, 328, 332, 341, 342, 344, 351, 362, 406, and 414, 447, 458 (index pages).

G

Materials Pertaining to the Arapaho in the Holdings of Thomas Gilcrease Institute of American History and Art

The following entries pertaining to the Arapaho are from The Gilcrease-Hargrett Catalogue of Imprints compiled by Lester Hargrett and published by University of Oklahoma Press (Norman, OK) in 1972. The items listed below in chronological order are in the collection of the Thomas Gilcrease Institute of American History and Art in Tulsa, Oklahoma (1400 North 25 West Avenue, Tulsa, OK 74127).

Hancock, W. S. Reports of Major General W. S. Hancock upon Indian Affairs, with Accompanying Exhibits. Washington: McGill & Witherow, [1867]. 133 p. 23 cm. Printed wrappers.
An extremely rare and valuable detailed report on Cheyenne, Sioux, Kiowa, Comanche and Arapahoe hostilities.

Miles, John D. Notice. [Darlington, 1880.] Broadside. 20.5 cm.
A warning to legal residents of the Cheyenne and Arapahoe Reservation not to harbor returning intruders recently expelled. Unrecorded, and the only known copy.

Miles, John D. Notice to Stockmen! [Darlington, 1882.] Broadside. 25 cm.
Notice by the Cheyenne and Arapahoe agent that intruders upon the Indian lands will be ejected. Unrecorded, and the only known copy.

Message from the President of the United States transmitting a Communication from the Secretary of the Interior of the 4th instant submitting Draft of Bill "to confirm the Title to Certain Land in the Indian Territory to the Cheyennes and Arapahoes, and the Wichitas and Affiliated Bands, to provide for the Issuance of Patents therefor." [Washington, 1883.] 82 p. 23 cm. Caption title. 2 folded maps.
The maps are exceptionally interesting and valuable.

Colby, L. W. Juan Jose Herrera vs. The United States and Arapahoe Indians. Defendants' Request for Findings of Fact. Objections to Findings of Fact requested by Claimant. Brief and Argument of Counsel for the Defense. [Washington, 1883.] 17 p. 23 cm. Wrapper title.
An interesting claim for the value of mules, horses, and oxen stolen from Herrera by Arapahoe Indians in Wyoming in 1870.

[Proclamation of President Cleveland ordering cattlemen off the Cheyenne and Arapahoe Reservation. Washington, 1885.] 2 p. 34 cm. Printed in script.

Before the Honorable Lucius Fairchild, Alfred M. Wilson, Warren D. Sayre, United States Commissioners, authorized to Negotiate with Certain Indians by Act of Congress approved March 2, 1889. Brief and Argument, Samuel J. Crawford, Attorney for the Cheyenne and Arapahoe Tribes. Washington: Wm. H. Moore, [1890]. 22 p. 23 cm. Wrapper title.

Message from the President of the United States, transmitting a Letter of the Secretary of the Interior with an Agreement by the Cherokee Commission with the Cheyenne and Arapahoe Indians for the Cession of Certain Lands. [Washington, 1890.] 24 p. 23 cm. Caption title.

Agreement with Cheyenne and Arapahoe Indians. [Washington, 1891.]   5 p.   22.5 cm.
Caption title.

Shellabarger & Wilson.   West Reno City vs. Persie Snowden and Rosa Goenawein. [Wash-
ington, 1896.]   25 p.   24 cm.   Caption title.
An interesting land dispute which grew out of the Cheyenne and Arapahoe Run of
April 19, 1892.

Everts, Hattie A.   Cheyenne and Arapahoe Work at the Watonga Mission. [Watonga,
1898.]   [8] p.   14.5 cm.   Caption title.   Plain wrappers.
A crudely printed narrative of missionary labors among the Cheyennes and Arapahoes.
Apparently the only known copy.

Sanford, D. A., tr.   Tune: Missionary Hymn. [Bridgeport, Okla. 1899?]   Broadside.
19.5 cm.
A hymn translated into the Arapahoe language.   Excessively rare.

Christmas with the Cheyennes and Arapahoes. [Watonga, 1900?].   Broadside.   28 cm.
A highly interesting account by an anonymous missionary of a Cheyenne and Arapahoe
Christmas celebration.   Unrecorded, and the only known copy.

Seger, Neatha H.   Cheyennes and Arapahoes in Oklahoma.   Indian News Items (in Indian
English). [Geary, 1930.]   Broadside.   28 cm.   3 columns.
Headed: Enough for 4 installments. Use 1-4 each week.

H
Museums with Significant Collections of Arapaho Material Culture

The following information was obtained by writing to museums both in the United States and abroad, known for their holdings of objects of material culture from the various Plains Indian tribes, including the Arapaho. Undoubtedly, some museums and private collectors were missed by the survey; the listing below is therefore not to be considered definitive. Altogether, the museums and individuals included here possess some four thousand specimens of Arapaho material culture, and there are possibly at least as many extant Arapaho objects unaccounted for here.

The list of museums and individuals is arranged alphabetically by locality, with the nature of relevant holdings summarized in a short paragraph. As a rule, more detailed descriptions are available from museum curators upon request.

Beloit, WI: Logan Museum of Anthropology, Beloit College, Beloit, WI 53511. The collection consists of about 20 specimens of clothing and 25 other objects (pipes, bags, and the like) from both Southern and Northern Arapaho; the specimens were collected by Albert Green Heath and date from the late nineteenth and early twentieth centuries.

Berkeley, CA: Lowie Museum of Anthropology, University of California at Berkeley, Kroeber Hall, Bancroft Way and College Avenue, Berkeley, CA 94720. The collection consists of no more than 20 objects, primarily clothing, collected by several individuals between 1876 and 1941.

Berlin (West): Museum für Völkerkunde, Arnimallee 27, D-1000 Berlin 33 (Dahlem). The collection consists of 22 Arapaho objects collected by several individuals as early as 1872.

Cambridge, MA: Peabody Museum of Archaeology and Ethnology, Harvard University, 11 Divinity Avenue, Cambridge, MA 02138. Holdings consist of approximately 60 specimens representing all aspects of Arapaho culture, primarily from the Northern branch, collected by several individuals between the mid-nineteenth century and 1936.

Chicago, IL: Field Museum of Natural History, Roosevelt Road at Lake Shore Drive, Chicago, IL 60605-2496. The collection consists of approximately 800 Southern and Northern Arapaho objects of every kind, collected between 1880 and 1905 by George A. Dorsey, J. W. Hudson, Cleaver Warden, and General C. C. Augur.

Denver, CO: The Denver Art Museum, 100 West 14th Avenue Parkway, Denver, CO 80204. The collection consists of 106 Arapaho specimens, including 45 examples of beadwork, 20 leather objects, 13 quilled objects, 9 musical instruments, 6 fur and/or feather objects, and the like; the objects date between the 1850s and 1950s and come from various sources.

Denver, CO: Denver Museum of Natural History, City Park, Denver, CO 80205.
The collection consists of 88 objects, partly exhibited in Crane American
Indian Hall, including clothing, toys, weapons, horse gear, a ghost dance shirt,
and materials from the Barrett P. Tyler Collection from St. Michael's Mission
(Ethete, Wyoming).

London, England: Museum of Mankind, Burlington Gardens, London W1X 2EX.
The collection consists of five items, including a bonnet of Chief Yellow Calf
(a Northern Arapaho), collected in 1927.

Los Angeles, CA: Southwest Museum, P. O. Box 128, Los Angeles, CA 90042.
The collection consists of approximately 50 objects of material culture, from both
the Southern and Northern Arapaho, including moccasins, pipe bags, leggings, bags,
pouches, and rattles. In addition, the holdings include photographs and other
printed memorabilia.

Milwaukee, WI: Milwaukee Public Museum, 800 W. Wells Street, Milwaukee, WI 53233.
The collection consists of 20 Arapaho objects from various sources, mostly clothing
and ornaments, but also bows, spoons, quill flatteners, and a pipe.

New Haven, CT: Peabody Museum of Natural History, Yale University, New Haven, CT
06511.
The collection consists of no more than ten objects, including a pipe, bone flesher
handles, and beaded pouches; the artifacts, some of which were collected by George
Bird Grinnell, date for the most part from the second half of the last century.

New York, NY: American Museum of Natural History, Central Park West at 79th Street,
New York, NY 10024.
The collection consists of approximately 878 ethnographic specimens, representing
all aspects of Southern and Northern Arapaho material culture, for the most part
collected by A. L. Kroeber about 1900.

New York, NY: Museum of the American Indian, Heye Foundation, Broadway at 155th
Street, New York, NY 10032.
The collection consists of approximately 750 specimens representing all aspects of
Arapaho material culture from as early as the 1830s.

Ottawa, Ontario, Canada: National Museum of Man, Ottawa, Ontario, Canada K1A 0M8.
The collection consists of no more than five items, among them a pipe which once
belonged to Chief Lone Bear.

Philadelphia, PA: The University Museum of Archaeology/Anthropology, University of
Pennsylvania, 33rd and Spruce Streets, Philadelphia, PA 19104.
Holdings consist of sizeable collections assembled by Stewart Culin on the John
Wanamaker Expeditions of 1900-1903, and by Reverend H. R. Voth; some objects were
acquired through an exchange made with George Heye in 1919. The overall collection
comprises about 295 game objects; about 25 musical instruments; about 55 bags,
cases, and pouches; about 70 items of clothing; about 60 weapons; about 106 ritual
and ceremonial objects; about 68 ornaments; and several dozen miscellaneous items.

Phoenix, AZ: The Heard Museum, 22 East Monte Vista Road, Phoenix, AZ 85004.
The collection consists of about 25 items, of which eight were collected by the
staff of the Fred Harvey Company in the early 1900s.

Pittsburgh, PA: Carnegie Museum of Natural History, 5800 Baum Boulevard, Pittsburgh,
PA 15206.
The collection consists of nearly 200 undated objects, the majority of them from
the Fred Harvey Collection (177 specimens--mostly clothing, storage containers,
pipes, and the like), the remainder from various donors.

Rimrock, AZ: Paul Dyck's Plains Indian Collection (private), Rimrock, AZ 86335.
The collection consists of approximately 140 specimens, representing all aspects
of Southern and Northern Arapaho material culture, collected by several individuals.

<u>Salem, MA</u>: Peabody Museum, East India Square, Salem, MA 01970.
The collection consists of approximately 50 Arapaho objects, acquired between 1888 and 1950 and including dance whistles, various articles of clothing, paint bags, pipe bags, tobacco pouches, dolls, scalp, headdress, horn spoon, and saddle bag.

<u>Washington, DC</u>: National Museum of Natural History, Smithsonian Institution, Washington, DC   20560.
The collection consists of approximately 450 specimens from both Southern and Northern Arapaho and is representative of a broad range of material culture.   Among the most significant components are 126 items collected by Emile Granier in the Rocky Mountain region and purchased by the Smithsonian Institution in 1898; 56 items received from the estate of Victor Evans in 1938; 43 Southern Arapaho items collected by James Mooney between 1892 and 1906; and 36 Southern Arapaho items collected by H. R. Voth between 1882 and 1892.

<u>Zürich, Switzerland</u>: Indianer-Museum der Stadt Zürich, Feldstrasse 89, CH-8004 Zürich, Switzerland.
The collection consists of 13 specimens, for the most part moccasins and bags.